Playing with Fire

also published in association with Leap Confronting Conflict

Working with Gangs and Young People
A Toolkit for Resolving Group Conflict
Jessie Feinstein and Nia Imani Kuumba
ISBN 978 1 84310 447 6

Making a Leap – Theatre of Empowerment
A Practical Handbook for Creative Drama Work with Young People
Sara Clifford and Anna Herrmann
Foreword by Alec Davison
ISBN 978 1 85302 632 4

of related interest

Just Schools
A Whole School Approach to Restorative Justice
Belinda Hopkins
ISBN 978 1 84310 132 1

Just Care
Restorative Justice Approaches to Working with Children in Public Care
Belinda Hopkins
Foreword by Jonathan Stanley
ISBN 978 1 84310 981 5

What Have I Done?
A Victim Empathy Programme for Young People
Pete Wallis
With Clair Aldington and Marian Liebmann
Illustrated by Emily Wallis
ISBN 978 1 84310 979 2

Why Me?
A Programme for Children and Young People Who Have Experienced Victimization
Shellie Keen, Tracey Lott and Pete Wallis
ISBN 978 1 84905 097 5

Are You Okay?
A Practical Guide to Helping Young Victims of Crime
Pete Wallis
ISBN 978 1 84905 098 2

The Pocket Guide to Restorative Justice
Pete Wallis and Barbara Tudor
ISBN 978 1 84310 629 6

Playing with Fire

Training for Those Working with Young People in Conflict

Second Edition

Fiona Macbeth and Nic Fine

with *Jo Broadwood, Carey Haslam and Nik Pitcher*

Jessica Kingsley *Publishers*
London and Philadelphia

Extract by André Gide on p.18 is reproduced by permission of the Fondation Catherine Gide.
Diagram from Allport 1954 on p.144 is reproduced by permission of Perseus Books Group.
Exercises 6.2, 6.3 and 6.4 from Fisher *et al.* 1998 are reproduced by permission of Responding to Conflict.
Diagram from Acland 1990 on p.161 is reproduced by permission of Andrew Acland.

This second edition published in 2011
by Jessica Kingsley Publishers
116 Pentonville Road
London N1 9JB, UK
and
400 Market Street, Suite 400
Philadelphia, PA 19106, USA

www.jkp.com

First published in 1992 by the National Youth Agency
Reprinted in 1995 by New Society Publishers

Library of Congress Cataloging in Publication Data
Macbeth, Fiona.
Playing with fire : training for those working with young people in conflict
/ Fiona Macbeth and Nic Fine ; with Jo Broadwood, Carey Haslam and Nik
Pitcher. -- 2nd ed.
p. cm.
Rev. ed. of: Playing with fire : creative conflict resolution for young
adults / Fiona Macbeth & Nic Fine. 1995.
Includes bibliographical references.
ISBN 978-1-84905-184-2 (alk. paper)
1. Conflict management--Study and teaching. 2. Interpersonal conflict--
Study and teaching. 3. Young adults--Conduct of life--Study and teaching. I.
Fine, Nic. II. Broadwood, Jo. III. Haslam, Carey. IV. Pitcher, Nik. V. Title.
BF637.I48M33 2011
303.6'90835--dc22
2010043817

British Library Cataloguing in Publication Data
A CIP catalogue record for this book is available from the British Library

ISBN 978 1 84905 184 2

Printed and bound in Great Britain
by the MPG Books Group

Contents

FIRE AND CONFLICT

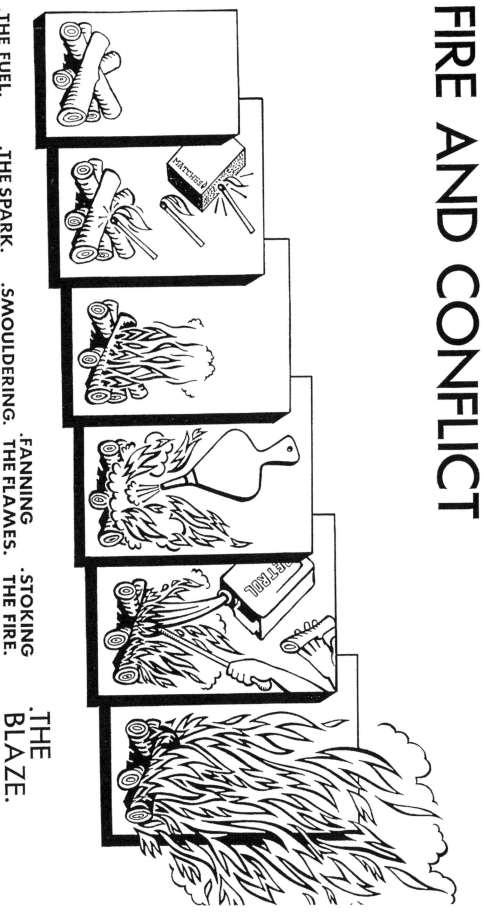

.THE FUEL.

.THE SPARK.

.SMOULDERING.

.FANNING THE FLAMES.

.STOKING THE FIRE.

.THE BLAZE.

Preface to the Second Edition

Playing with Fire is a resource manual and structured training programme for those practising or wishing to develop as youth and conflict practitioners or trainers.

It is particularly useful for professionals who work with young people, including youth, education, police, youth justice and prison services. It provides frameworks for understanding the causes and consequences of conflict, and shares practical exercises, strategies and techniques that develop skills and resources for working with youth and conflict issues.

The first edition of *Playing with Fire* was published in 1992. The original *Playing with Fire* was published as a structured training programme for developing youth and conflict practitioners. The original authors, Fi Macbeth and Nic Fine, researched the materials and frameworks drawing on best practice in youth and conflict work from the UK, the USA, Canada and Australia. For the first time in the UK those working with young people were provided with a framework for understanding youth conflict and some practical resources to work with it more constructively. Since 1992 the manual has sold over 10,000 copies worldwide.

Preventing youth violence and conflict is currently high on the political and national agenda in the UK. There have been a number of specific strategies and plans which have attempted to tackle this issue. There is also a high level of media interest in crimes involving young people, who are frequently depicted in the local and national press as dangerous and uncontrollable. At the same time there is an acknowledgement by many working in the field that there is a serious skills and confidence gap with those working with young people and issues of conflict and violence, and that youth professionals need to continue to develop their abilities in order to meet the current and emerging challenges.

Our opinion at Leap is that this work with young people is possibly more critical and necessary today than it was in 1992, when the first edition of this book was published. More youth practitioners are now engaged in delivering violence prevention programmes, and increased funding is invested in this methodology. Youth and conflict work has progressed significantly in the UK and it is now recognised as a specialism in its own right, with attendant qualifications from entry-level accreditation up to a specialist HE Certificate and Diploma.

This second edition contains much of the original content, still relevant and dependable core materials for understanding conflict, and tried and tested techniques for working constructively with it. New thinking and additional materials come from the learning acquired by Leap from ongoing hands-on delivery in schools, local communities and multi-agency partnerships around the UK. This is supported by considerable experience in running professional development courses and by the expertise involved in setting up a specialist academy and developing a suite of qualifications in the subject.

Leap Confronting Conflict now has a pool of over 50 specialist practitioners, all of whom are continually deepening their skills in the competencies that go to make up this specialism. The material in *Playing with Fire* is at the core of the content we use to develop our own specialists.

The exercises in the training programme have evolved in various ways. Some were developed through our own work and experiences in the field; others were adapted from ideas and materials that we came into contact with along the way. The original *Playing with Fire* was influenced by many ideas which were originally conceived by others, and we appreciatively acknowledge their contributions to the materials in this programme. We would like to give particular credit to the following people and organisations:

- Paulo Freire
- John Bergman and the Geese Theatre Company
- Augusto Boal
- Youth at Risk, formerly the Breakthrough Foundation
- Richard Cohen from School Mediation Associates
- Responding to Conflict
- The Alternatives to Violence Project.

We would like to acknowledge the many people who have supported and contributed to the work of Leap Confronting Conflict since 1987. Special mention must go to Alec Davison, the founder of Leap Confronting Conflict, who continues to be a huge inspiration for many of us; and Leap's senior trainers, Jassy Denison, Jessie Feinstein, Nia Imani Kuumba, Rene Manradge, Amanda Nelmes and Tony Weekes, who have done much over the years to develop the training of specialist practitioners.

Most importantly this book is dedicated to all the young people we have worked with: the young apprentices and volunteers, peer mediators and young trainers, the present and past participants of Leap's youth projects and training programmes. Their courage, passion and commitment to managing conflict in their own lives and the lives of their communities creatively and constructively is an inspiration.

About the authors

Fiona Macbeth is currently a Teaching Fellow in Applied Drama at the University of Exeter, specialising in training students for work with youth at risk. Nic Fine now lives in South Africa where he is the director of Hearts of Men, an NGO running community-based mentoring interventions with young men at risk. Jo Broadwood is a founder and director of Talking Communities, a community-interest company specialising in working with community conflict. Until 2010 she was part of the leadership team at Leap, where she set up the Leap Academy of Youth and Conflict, and is a Leap senior trainer. Carey Haslam and Nik Pitcher are Leap senior trainers. All are specialist youth and conflict practitioners with many years of experience.

This programme has been trademarked and Leap Confronting Conflict has copyright of this programme and materials. Leap is happy for this material to be used in an educational context but asks that you please clearly credit Leap as the source.

Introduction

How to use this manual

The structure of the manual follows the development of a conflict, using fire as an analogy, with the exercises grouped accordingly. However, it is possible to regroup and reorder the materials for a different focus (see below). You will notice that the exercises gradually become more demanding. The later ones ask more of the participants and of the facilitators; they require that trust has been established within the group and that a safe training environment has been created. The early exercises will help to establish this atmosphere of trust and group cohesion. The later sections assume you have already done some of this preparatory work and have built up sufficient levels of trust and communication in the group to undertake deeper exploration and reflection.

Leap Confronting Conflict most often delivers the course as a ten-day training programme over three long weekends spanning a three-month period, and in the next chapter we set out how to do that. Alternatively you could organise the course around conflict themes, such as anger; enemies and enemy thinking; identity and prejudice; and power and powerlessness. Some programmes may work better grouped around themes of single-sex or single-identity work. Detailed session plans for both the ten-day course and themed sessions are laid out at the back of the book in Appendix A.

You can also choose to dip in and out of this manual, taking materials for use in your own training courses and sessions. We would still strongly recommend that you read 'Preparing the Ground' and 'Guidance for Trainers'. The ideas and techniques shared in these two chapters have been developed over nearly 20 years' experience of training youth work professionals in youth and conflict skills, and are a reliable resource for any trainer embarking on delivering this work.

Conflict: danger and opportunity

The characters that make up the word 'conflict' in Chinese are *danger* and *opportunity*. This programme works on the understanding that there is potential for growth and positive change in any conflict.

Conflict is not necessarily destructive – in fact it is a vital part of life and often drives valuable growth and change. Conflict becomes damaging when it is ignored or repressed, or when the only responses to it are to bully, bulldoze, fight or withdraw. Destructive conflict is often linked to feelings of social isolation or exclusion, to being under-resourced emotionally and practically, to not being heard or valued. The programme offers a structure within which participants can explore situations of conflict and potential violence, primarily in their work with young people, practise skills for dealing with them, and rehearse possible strategies and techniques for future use.

The fire analogy

From the beginning of the experimental work that led to the evolution of this programme, there was an attempt to encourage young people to see the work of confronting conflict as something daring, exciting and challenging. It takes great courage to step into conflict with the aim of resolving it constructively. Conflicts can release overwhelming personal energies, and it is a brave person who intervenes when the situation is ablaze. Young people found the firefighter a more robust and identifiable image than the peacemaker, and the work soon took off using the fire analogy as a simple way of enabling young people to see how conflict escalates. The analogy can facilitate a memorable and quick analysis of the stages of escalating conflict, which, like fire, is a good servant and a bad master.

Like fire, conflict has the energy and power to heat and to hurt. Conflict and fire grow in much the same way and are both potentially dangerous. When harnessed, however, fire can provide warmth and energy; when confronted, conflict can facilitate both personal and social change. Just as fires have incendiaries, fanners and stokers, so conflicts have the embittered, provokers and agitators. For positive transformation they clearly need listeners, persisters and mediators. Positive transformation is always possible. This programme is underpinned by the understanding that there is both a destructive and a creative potential in fire and in conflict. A schematic application of the analogy, in both its negative and its positive dimensions, is laid out opposite.

Values and core principles

Embodied in this work is the idea of individual respect, the principle that every human life is valuable. We need to be able to respect ourselves; we need to respect others. We all want and deserve to be heard and to be fairly treated. This is the message of the programme and therefore underlies its conduct and process.

There is a disposition within this work towards non-violence. Behind it lies recognition of the fact that unfairness, injustice and lack of basic resources tend to provoke conflict, which in turn can escalate into violence. Oppression, tyranny and imperialism may seem to leave no alternative but violence in the face of suffering, brutality and conquest. But violence will always leave legacies of hurt, bitterness, vengefulness and destruction, and can bring bloodshed and death which may never be forgiven. Violence diminishes the violent as well as the victim. This programme argues that in our personal conflicts violence and disempowerment can be avoided if alternative behaviour has been rehearsed and prepared for.

Running through all of Leap's work there is a belief in the potential within all young people whatever their circumstances. In a world where young people are increasingly seen as a problem Leap works from a perspective which champions young people as the solution and supports their potential to be leaders in preventing and resolving conflict, from helping sort out a disagreement in a friendship to co-mediating alongside adults in a community setting. As adults working with young people this course will help prepare us to meet the challenges and tests young people set us, so that we can fully support them in developing their full potential.

Fire: conflict and change

Conflict

PEOPLE

Whenever people are in contact with each other, there is potential for conflict. This potential will vary according to the different degrees of combustibility in the individuals.

INCIDENT

There are always tensions and disagreements between people. Some of them can cause a spark which ignites conflict.

BROODING

Tensions and grievances are smouldering away but are unexpressed. The conflict feeds off rumour and gossip.

AGGRAVATION

Those who are interested in agitating the situation provoke it further. Feelings of anger and hurt may be expressed as prejudice and hate.

ESCALATION

The situation is intensified by the outside pressures of the social environment. Prejudice and disaffection add to the conflict.

CONSEQUENCES

There is a blazing conflict in which some people are damaged. No-one involved is untouched by it.

Fire

THE FUEL

The raw material of the fire. Some of it is highly combustible. Some of it is damp and flame-resistant.

THE SPARK

Friction causes sparks to fly. Some land on dry wood and it catches light.

SMOULDERING

The fuel catches light and begins to smoke. There is an indication of fire.

FANNING THE FLAMES

The wind blows and the smouldering fuel flickers with life. The flames lick and leap.

STOKING THE FIRE

The fire consumes the fuel. It demands more. Huge logs are piled onto the fire.

THE BLAZE

The fire rages. It is a huge blaze. It will not die down easily.

Change

PEOPLE

Whenever people are in contact with one another, there is potential for challenge and growth. Different values, opinions or aims contain raw issues and fuel for fire.

FLASH OF INSIGHT

There are always raw issues in a community or relationship. Sometimes a flash of new insight can bring an issue alive for an individual.

TENTATIVE RESPONSE

The individual looks for shared concern from others, making an initial response to the issue.

ENCOURAGED ACTION

Those showing concern for the issue grow in number, encouraging and supporting each other.

INCREASED RESPONSE

Response to the issue increases. The possibilities of achievement inspire action from many.

EFFECTIVE ACTION

Aims are achieved. People celebrate the blazing fire. It is a beacon which lights, warms and inspires.

The principle of Developing Potential is one of four which underpin all of Leap's work. These four key principles – Developing Potential, Being Responsible, Creating Communication and Building Community – are the foundation stones on which all Leap programmes are developed and all Leap facilitation and training work is based. They are both aspirational and practical, reflected in the conduct of our frontline practitioners and delivery teams, but also evident throughout the organisation in structures and procedures, and in our behaviour towards each other and those we come into contact with on behalf of the organisation.

Lastly this work believes in the essential creative potential within each individual. We are born with an urge to play and create, to be curious and inventive, to experiment and to explore; it stays with us from cradle to grave. Our upbringing and education either affirm and legitimise that urge or smother it. With caring support, good encouragement and new opportunities, creativity can be nurtured and can flourish into more positive human relations and enhanced personal well-being. The programme trusts that change and growth will come as creativity is released, and that such release is possible, in some degree, for every one of us. Confronting conflict is about tough love and keeping on believing that change is possible.

The learning experience

This is an experiential learning course. The learning process follows Kolb's Cycle of Experiential Learning (1984): learners participate in exercises, reflect on their experience, then use these reflections to formulate new understandings. Frameworks and models are fed in and tested in action through the exercises. Participants take this learning and test it for themselves in real-life situations. In this model reflection is as important as experience. The course materials are rich in opportunities for experience; it is the facilitator's responsibility to ensure there are sufficient opportunities for reflection and that participants are encouraged to try out techniques in real life and bring back the learning to the group.

Each exercise is presented with a short description which outlines the focus and the methodology used. The description is then broken down into aims with specific areas of learning. The directions are a step-by-step guide to running the exercise, and the feedback and discussion section gives ideas for questions to enable and encourage reflection on the experience of the exercise. Additional useful points for facilitators regarding the delivery and the concepts being explored are detailed in the notes. The last section details which specific skills are utilised and developed in the exercise.

A key focus in this course is on the participants examining their own relationship to conflict so that they can be a better resource and role-model for the young people they work with. In order to do that they need to practise using the tools and frameworks on areas in their own lives where they struggle, including in their work with young people. Experiencing our own struggle with our own 'learning edge', seeing how the skills we use or don't use in our personal and professional lives are interrelated, and observing how we are supported and facilitated to move beyond destructive conflict, will resource us when we are supporting young people in their own learning.

The emphasis on examining our own thoughts, feelings, interpretations and habits in conflict situations may provoke discomfort in some participants. An important distinction to make is that the course may be therapeutic at times but it is not therapy. The critical emphasis should always be on producing better-resourced role-models and workers for young people. The side benefits may be new skills and understandings that participants can apply in their personal lives, but the main focus is on the benefit to young people of more skilled workers.

There will be many opportunities during the training for participants to put forward themselves and their own work situations as case studies so that the group can experience the application of the tools and frameworks offered to real situations. When these opportunities arise the group can choose the situation that resonates most with them. In this way the learning needs of both the individual and the group can be met.

The work needs to be guided with confidence and skill in order to establish and maintain a safe environment in which challenge and change are possible. Leap always delivers this programme with a team of at least two facilitators/trainers. This provides a richer and safer learning experience for participants. Where possible the facilitator team should reflect something of the diversity of the world we live in. In this way the facilitators can model not only a skilful approach to working with challenge and conflict, but also a respectful co-working relationship across differences of gender, age, sexuality, ethnicity or culture.

Facilitators should be open, warm, accepting and positive, and act as careful trustees of a safe and supportive learning environment for the group. The programme is therefore best delivered by trainers who are skilled and experienced in leading group work and facing the challenges and rewards of both group dynamics and conflict issues. Strategies for facilitating this work are developed further in the sections entitled 'Preparing the Ground' and 'Guidance for Trainers'.

In delivering this programme you need to be confident in your ability to both train and facilitate. Your ability to facilitate dialogue around difficult issues and conflict situations will be as important as your ability to support others to learn concepts, tools and skills for handling conflict more creatively and constructively, so throughout the manual we use the words trainer and facilitator interchangeably, as you need to be competent in both areas.

In 'Preparing the Ground' and 'Guidance for Trainers' we give detailed guidance on how to structure and run an intensive 'Playing with Fire' training programme.

Preparing the Ground

Preparing the Ground – for change, for challenge, for growth

Preparing the Ground is the detailed work of preparation and planning which means that by the time the participants walk into the room they are already engaged and focused on the journey ahead. For the training team it is about establishing or renewing a strong co-facilitation relationship, imagining what kind of journey might lie ahead and what some of the inspirations and challenges might be along the way.

Focus

Course structure; practicalities; preparing as trainers; preparing participants.

Course structure

Leap most often structures the programme as a ten-day training over three long weekends. This provides an intense experience for participants with plenty of time for reflection in between, and for incorporating new skills and knowledge into practice between sessions.

The three weekends are organised around the themes of *Me in Conflict*, *You and Me in Conflict* and *You, Me and Others in Conflict*.

Me in conflict

> Anyone can become angry – that is easy. But to be angry with the right person, to the right degree, at the right time, for the right reasons, and in the right way – that is not easy.
>
> *Aristotle*

This is about intervening in our own thoughts and emotions – that is, what goes on inside us – with the aim of taking more control of our reactions and responses to difficult situations and potential conflicts.

You and me in conflict

> One does not discover new oceans without consenting to lose sight of the shore for a very long time.
>
> *André Gide*

This is about intervening within an interaction with another person or group, with the aim of being assertive about our personal needs and perceptions. It is also about intervening between another person and what is going on for them internally (for example, when they are expressing bigotry or hatred), with the aim of expiating their underlying emotions and needs (for example, looking at their own 'enemy' within themselves).

You, me and others in conflict

> Peace is not the absence of war. It is not a passive state of being. We must wage peace as vigilantly as we wage war.
>
> *The 14th Dalai Lama*

> If you cannot bear the smoke, you will never get to the fire.
>
> *Wodaabe proverb*

This is about intervening as a third party between individuals or groups involved in a dispute, with the aim of enabling the disputants to come to a mutually acceptable resolution. This theme will also explore roles and actions for social change.

Practicalities

The physical environment

The physical environment in which sessions take place is important. You will need to think about noise levels and privacy – it is better to have a private space that is not used by others for access and where it is possible to work uninterrupted and leave papers and materials overnight. The size of the space is important – it needs to be big enough to accommodate the group comfortably with plenty of room for moving around and doing active work. It may also be useful to have some smaller break-out rooms for when the group divides into smaller groups for particular activities. Lighting and heating is important so that the working environment is as comfortable as possible – natural lighting is always better, as are fresh air in summer and sufficient heating in winter.

Establish whether the working space is going to be used for eating and drinking during working hours or in breaks. It is always better to have an alternative space for participants to relax in between sessions. This means that there is a clear distinction between 'work' and 'non-work' space.

If participants are staying away from home in order to be able to attend the course then giving them information about where banks, post offices, shops, local eateries and so on are situated will help them feel welcomed and looked after.

On the first day we would always recommend that the training team get there at least an hour early so that they can welcome the first participants. It will also give trainers time to check the venue is arranged as desired and to make any last-minute adjustments to training plans.

Equipment and resources

Essential resources are a flipchart (or large sheets of paper and a supply of Blu-tack™), marker pens, scrap paper and pens. It is good to have at least one wall on which large sheets of paper, wallcharts and visual aids can be displayed. This area needs to be well lit. As most of this course is experiential there is little need for much technical equipment such as projector, computer, etc.

The exercises require minimal preparation of materials. Some will require handouts to be photocopied or stimulus cards to be prepared. Any items necessary for suggested games (blindfold, beanbags and so on) are readily available.

Size of group

Group numbers for this kind of work can be between 6 and 18. Intimacy is important. A group of 18 with 2 facilitators is probably the absolute maximum size for this kind of work. The optimum group size is 12 to 14. A circle is an effective structure for general group work. The sightlines are good, and it provides a feeling of equality and security for the participants.

Preparing as trainers

As a trainer and facilitator in conflict resolution participants will be looking to you to lead by example and will be observing you closely to see how you deal with the challenges of facilitating and supporting individual and group learning around conflict. There will inevitably be moments when you get hooked as a facilitator or brought up against your own learning edge by a question or a challenge from a participant. How you deal with these will be a huge learning experience both for participants and for you!

We suggest that you need to be mentally and emotionally prepared to run the course. Ideally you should be in a stable emotional state and not experiencing any distressing or unexpected life-changing events. You should yourself have undergone some training in this work so that you are familiar with the content and aware of what it can raise for participants.

A team of at least two facilitators is always a good idea. There are many advantages to this: mutual support, continuity, a balance of different styles and strengths, the sharing of preparation and facilitation tasks, the possibility of working simultaneously with two small groups and, of course, the opportunity to demonstrate a model of teamwork and cooperation.

It is important that as a team you schedule in plenty of time for planning the programme. This will include clarifying and discussing ways to achieve the aims and the learning outcomes, agreeing the content, timings, preparation of materials and who is leading what. We would also suggest that you take time during the planning stage to discuss your working relationship.

You may want to discuss areas of strength and weakness in relation to the course content and levels of facilitation skills, your individual hopes and fears for the course and new challenges you would like to set yourself, and share openly any concerns or anxieties you may have about working with each other or delivering the training. You will also want to agree the co-facilitation relationship you will model to participants, particularly in relation to working across difference, working with challenge and conflict in the training room, equality, mutual respect and skilful communication. You may also want to discuss and agree in advance what you will do if conflict and challenge emerge in the relationship between you, and how you will support yourselves and each other in that case.

Your role as facilitators and trainers

At Leap we see the role of the trainer/facilitator as follows:

- To introduce and guide participants through exercises and activities that will facilitate their learning around conflict, according to the aims and objectives of the course and specific exercises. This will include:
  - giving clear instructions and guidelines
  - facilitating reflections, share-backs and discussions
  - maintaining the pace and flow of sessions
  - managing time, for example, setting definite time limits on tasks, discussions and reflections
  - negotiating and extending time where necessary rather than running over time with no clarity or sense of purpose.
- To support participants in maintaining a safe and supportive learning environment that will enable individual and group learning. This will include:
  - asking questions to support participants' learning
  - saying what you see and hear
  - reflecting back what you've heard
  - giving feedback on personal challenges and goals
  - linking what is happening in the room to conflict theory and practice
  - monitoring and paying attention to group dynamics
  - creating a learning environment where everything that happens is useful.

It is important that difficulties between participants or between participants and a facilitator do not get ignored, stored or buried. Difficulties in group dynamics can be viewed as a golden opportunity to deepen our understanding of conflict, its causes, roots and consequences. The section 'Guidance for Trainers' contains useful recommendations and tips for working constructively with conflict and challenging behaviour if it is displayed by participants.

The section 'Games and Group Discussion Techniques' outlines some techniques for getting problems into the open and working effectively with them.

We would strongly recommend you set aside time at the end of each day to review the day properly with your co-trainer, share any observations, concerns and reflections on individual participants, the course content, facilitation issues or your working relationship; and to discuss and if necessary adjust the plans for the next day.

Preparing participants

Before a course we recommend pre-course questionnaires be sent out, and returned in time for the training team's first planning session. These will help the participant to focus on what they want to get out of the course and encourage them to set clear personal and professional goals for themselves. The training team can also identify early on if the participant's overall expectations and learning needs are in line with the course content and aims. If necessary they can call participants to clarify and discuss their expectations or any worries they have.

Because of the intensity of the course methodology it is desirable that participants also be in a stable emotional and mental state when undertaking the programme. *Playing with Fire* is not a therapy programme and is not intended as a place for participants to work out intense conflicts or problems that they are currently experiencing. If it is apparent from an application form or pre-course questionnaire that any of the above may be an issue for a participant then one of the training team should call them and discuss this further, including, if necessary, the appropriateness of them participating in the programme at this time.

The questionnaire is also an opportunity for participants to flag up if they have any disabilities or particular learning or support needs so that trainers can plan for this and adapt exercises and activities so that everyone can participate fully.

Gaining a firm commitment from participants to attend all parts of the programme is also important. Regular attendance helps build trust and stability in the group and is vital to this kind of work. Exploring issues around attendance, timekeeping and so on can be an interesting conversation for participants as it helps them reflect on working with young people on these same issues.

Chapter 1
The Fuel
Ourselves and Our Communication

The raw material of the fire lies still. Piles of dead wood and scattered coals cover the earth. The dead dry wood is combustible; the coals can withstand heat a little longer. Some of the wood is still damp, and flame-resistant to some degree; the treated wood is highly resistant. The raw materials of the fire are constantly changing; dead wood disintegrates, new wood grows, coals form and all is movement. The raw material of the fire lies still but alive.

There is potential for conflict within us and around us all the time. Life and conflict are inextricably linked. Conflict is part of life and growth. Without conflict there would be no change and no challenge. Where energies meet there is movement and potential opposition, challenge and change.

By building an awareness of ourselves and those around us as fuel for violent conflict, we can discover productive alternatives to a damaging blaze. There is creative potential in conflict, just as there is potential in fire for warmth and energy as well as destruction. Developing self-awareness and communication skills are ways of working on the potential for challenge and growth in conflict, rather than allowing it to fester through lack of attention and awareness.

Focus

Personal histories; definitions of conflict; people as the fuel for conflict; how people communicate; characteristics of effective communication.

Key concepts

Conflict: understanding, meaning; awareness: personal histories, self-awareness, awareness of others; communication: body language, interpretation, listening, expression.

Key questions

To what extent does self-awareness determine our response in situations of conflict? How do our overall communication skills relate to our behaviour in conflict situations? To what extent does our understanding of others determine how successful we are when attempting to resolve conflict?

The Fuel

1.1	Personal Road Maps	45 min.
1.2	Letter to an Alien: Conflict is...?	35 min.
1.3	Punchy Proverbs	35 min.
1.4	Conflict Line-up	35 min.
1.5	Testing the Water	25 min.
1.6	Four Word Build	30 min.
1.7	Back-to-back Listening	20 min.
1.8	Countdown	20 min.
1.9	Attention Zones	35 min.
1.10	What Language Do You Speak?	25 min.
1.11	Open and Closed	20 min.
1.12	Reading the Face	25 min.

Exercise 1.1 Personal Road Maps

Time: 45 min.

Description

An individual and group exercise in which participants share the important moments of their lives with the group.

Aims

For participants to be specific about the key events and influences in their lives and to share them with the group.

Directions

1. Each participant needs a large sheet of paper. Ask the participants to design a road map that shows the paths and routes they have taken during their lifetime. They should have a choice of whatever colours they require. They can draw signposts at various points to indicate crossroads, hazards, traffic lights, hairpin bends, clear straight roads or other landmarks. **10 min.**

2. Participants divide into pairs. Each participant shares their map with their partner, who says what they can gather from the drawing. The drawer can then feed back. They swap over. **10 min.**

3. An extension of the exercise could be for one participant to enact their journey for the rest of the group. The floor of the working space now becomes the map surface and the participant traces their footsteps to show the shape of their journey. They could enlist other members of the group to represent the road signs in tableaux. The group can give feedback about what they learned from the presentation. **15 min.**

Feedback and discussion

What common threads do participants see in their own lives and the lives of others? Has tracing the map been personally useful? If so, how? How does what they learned help them in their understanding of others? **10 min.**

Notes

The format of the map can be a useful device for exploring complex emotions and events. Participants can use their maps as a 'touchstone' which they refer back to throughout the course. They might add additional material learned through further exercises; for example, they might highlight moments of conflict; identify 'bombs' and 'shields' or 'triggers' in those conflicts; or distinguish the facts or interpretations of key experiences. They could put the key characters from their lives into the maps. Key incidents could be re-enacted using role-play or films. Participants could also consider where the next part of the journey might take them and add this to the existing map.

Skills

Ability to visualise. Spatial awareness. Clarity. Interpretation.

Exercise 1.2 Letter to an Alien: Conflict is…?

Time: 35 min.

Description

A large-group exercise exploring the meaning of the word 'conflict'.

Aims

To clarify what we mean by conflict. To discover the range of responses within the group. To work towards a group definition of conflict.

Directions

1. Divide a large sheet of paper into columns, each headed by a letter of the alphabet. For the purposes of this exercise choose letters A to H.

2. Ask participants to wordstorm conflict words. The group should try to provide at least one word for each letter (for example, A-anger, B-broken and so on). The words can be written down by a nominated scribe as they are called out or simply added to the chart by individual participants. There is no debate or questioning at this stage about why certain words have been chosen.   **5 min.**

3. Once the chart is completed (it's good to have a strict time limit), people can ask each other questions about their chosen words – what certain words mean, how they are connected with conflict, and so forth. But no judgements are to be passed.   **3 min.**

4. Participants then split into pairs or groups of three and select a letter from the chart. (It is best if each pair or group has a different letter.) They then draft a short communication to an extraterrestrial alien who has never heard of conflict, explaining what it is. Each group should use the words listed under their letter. The communications are then shared with the whole group.   **10 min.**

5. Mixing participants into new groups of four or five, ask each group to create a brief definition of conflict in the form of a slogan. These could all start with 'Conflict is…'. An additional activity requiring extra time is for each group to think of an imaginative way to present their definition. They could use tableaux, involving everyone in the presentation.   **10 min.**

Feedback and discussion

Back in the whole group, participants are invited to reflect on what they have learnt about conflict from this exercise. How has their understanding changed? Do they see conflict as positive or negative? It can also be useful to focus on their experience of the interaction between members of their group. How did the group draft its letter to the alien? How did the group agree upon its definition? Was it easy to get to a slogan on conflict?   **7 min.**

Notes

Leap takes a broad definition of conflict, and the work of the manual will focus on both internal conflicts (those we have in our heads) and external conflicts (those we have with other people). It might be useful to refer to 'Conflict: danger and opportunity' in the Introduction to the manual (p.13).

Participants could be invited to develop their definitions of conflict over the period of the whole course. These should evolve as the subject is explored in greater depth. It might be useful, at the end of the course, to see if the whole group can agree on a final common definition.

Skills

Literacy. Group interaction. Group devising.

Exercise 1.3 Punchy Proverbs

Time: 35 min.

Description

A small-group exercise exploring the effects of violence and violent behaviour.

Aims

To generate debate on the use of violence against others and its effects. To encourage the group to express their personal opinions on the subject. To involve the group in bringing to life a proverb.

Directions

1.   Divide the participants into groups of three or four. Using cards prepared in advance, give each group a proverb that deals with some aspect of violent behaviour. Add your own discoveries to these two African examples:

      When two elephants fight, it is the grass that suffers most.

      The axe forgets; the log does not.

2.   Each group work out an interpretation of their proverb. What does it mean to them? What circumstances might it be referring to? Can the group think of concrete situations? The results of small-group work are then fed back to the whole group. If the small-group are unanimous in their understanding, then one member could feed back. If not, the group must decide who says what. It is valuable at this stage to see the variety of interpretations and responses.   **10 min.**

3.   The small groups are now asked to choose a way of visualising their proverb, as a tableau or a series of tableaux.   **10 min.**

4.   Invite each group to exhibit their tableau to the other participants. Ask each figure in the image to say what they are feeling or thinking. Participants observing the tableau should explore what they see and guess at what the proverb could be before the text is shared. If there is time, this tableau could now be developed into a short dramatic scene which might deepen everyone's understanding of the proverb.   **5 min.**

Feedback and discussion

Is there stored wisdom or stored prejudice in the proverbs? Do the sayings need to be challenged? Discussion of the origins of such sayings can be valuable. Do the group know any other proverbs or sayings that refer to situations of violence or conflict? You might suggest that they ask friends, parents, grandparents or people in the community from different cultural backgrounds for any relevant sayings or proverbs, and then display these on the walls over future sessions.   **10 min.**

Notes

Participants could decide to develop their own sayings. These might be worked on and shared over later weeks or months. It could be useful to look at a variety of sayings dealing with different issues related to the course's themes. You might find it necessary to explore and discuss some of the issues raised in the tableaux or dramatic scenes, especially those to do with violence or conflict in the family.

Skills

Interpretation. Dialogue. Imagination. Dramatising. Teamwork.

Exercise 1.4 Conflict Line-up

Time: 35 min.

Description

A group exercise in which individuals identify their automatic reaction to conflict and where that reaction comes from.

Aims

To identify our instinctual or gut reaction to personal, interpersonal and familial conflicts. To explore how our early lessons and role-models in handling conflict affect how we deal with conflict now. To identify differences in the way we deal with conflict with different people.

Directions

1. Tell participants that this exercise explores their automatic reaction to conflict – their gut instinct – so they should not over-analyse their responses. Set up an imaginary line across the room. The ends of the line represent *fight* or *flight*, with participants moving along the line in reaction to a question or examples of personal conflicts.   **2 min.**

2. Ask participants to consider the following question: 'When a conflict arises are you the kind of person who wants to flee – leave the room or retreat inside – or fight – get verbally or physically involved in the conflict?' Ask individuals to place themselves on the line and ask three or four volunteers to say why they have put themselves where they are. Participants may want to move in response to what they hear from others.   **5 min.**

3. You can also use more specific examples, such as a disagreement with a partner; a disagreement with a parent/family member; or a disagreement with a boss/someone in authority, etc.   **5 min.**

4. Create an imaginary triangle in the room, where each point represents one of the following ways of dealing with conflict: *Talk and Sort*; *Hidden and Silent*; *Out and Shout*. Ask participants to place themselves on the point of the triangle that most fits their experience of how conflict was dealt with when they were growing up, whether it was in a family or in the care system. You might ask three or four participants with different experiences:

    What was conflict like growing up?

    > How did the adults around you deal with it?

    > How did you and/or your siblings deal with it?

    > What was your role in the family?   **5 min.**

5. Finally ask participants to move to the point of the triangle where they would put themselves now and ask them why.   **3 min.**

6. A further extension to this is 'hotspots'. Place a piece of paper on the floor in the centre of the room. The paper represents the conflict situations listed below. Work through the situations listed. Ask participants to place themselves physically on the triangle in

relation to each situation, or in another position in the room which represents their approach to the situation.

The conflict is between:

- two young people whom you don't know
- two young people, one of whom you don't know
- two young people, one of whom you don't like
- two colleagues at work
- two friends
- two people on the street.

Choose whether the conflicts are verbal or physical. You can be creative with the scenarios, stipulating variations in age, gender, ethnicity and positions of authority, depending on the needs of the group. Again ask three or four people to say why they placed themselves where they did. **5 min.**

Feedback and discussion

How can knowing our instinctual reaction to conflict support us? Can you see a link between your past and how you presently deal with conflict? Do you notice any similarities or differences in how you deal with conflict compared with your parents or carers? What are they? What other factors affect your approach to conflict? **10 min.**

Notes

Reflecting on childhood experiences can bring up strong emotions for some participants; if this is the case it might be useful for everyone to spend some time in pairs discussing their experience of the exercise before the feedback. This exercise is a useful warm-up to Exercise 2.4, 'Red Flags'.

Skills

Listening. Self-reflection. Clear communication. Emotional awareness.

Exercise 1.5 Testing the Water

Time: 25 min.

Description

An individual exercise in personal reflection about how participants approach situations.

Aims

To encourage participants to reflect on their most common patterns of behaviour. To look at how our behaviour varies according to changes in circumstances.

Directions

1. Ask participants to imagine they are arriving at the seaside. Set the scene by marking out the beach and the sea across the room using masking tape. The participants should be on the beach. Ask them: 'If you are at the seaside, which is the most likely way for you to get into the water?'

    ◦ Just run towards the sea and dive in.

    ◦ Walk in slowly, wetting your body bit by bit and getting used to the temperature.

    ◦ Dip your toe in the water, then decide if you'll go in.

    ◦ Stand on the beach contemplating the view and surroundings, and considering what you will do next.

    ◦ Do something else.   **2 min.**

2. Ask them to position themselves according to their most likely way of behaving and say why they have put themselves there.   **3 min.**

3. Once everyone in the group has chosen their positions, give each type of response a title such as 'plunger', 'wader', 'tester', 'procrastinator'. Discuss the positive and negative attributes of each of these types of behaviour.   **5 min.**

4. Now ask each participant to consider whether the mode of behaviour they originally chose is their most common way of behaving generally, particularly in new situations. If they find that they behave differently in different circumstances, get them to describe a particular situation and a response. Once they have thought about this, they could share their thoughts in groups of three or so.   **5 min.**

Feedback and discussion

Do we have a habitual way of behaving in new situations? How does our behaviour change in different circumstances? What sort of conflicts could arise when a 'plunger' has to work alongside a 'tester'? In what ways could the two actually benefit one another? What are the positive aspects of each approach? For what reasons do people adopt these different approaches?

10 min.

Notes

The assumption here is that a greater awareness of how we react in different situations increases our understanding of the dynamics involved in conflict situations. It also encourages attention to the behaviour of others and an understanding of the needs underlying their behaviour. This exercise is a useful lead-in to developing personal challenges (see 'Guidance for Trainers').

Skills

Self-awareness. Awareness of types of behaviour.

Exercise 1.6 Four Word Build

Time: 30 min.

Description

An exercise involving work in pairs, small groups and large groups, which is designed to promote discussion and the exchange of opinions.

Aims

To identify what the group considers the most important aspects of a given theme. To try to establish a group consensus in prioritising key concepts of the theme. To promote an ethos of participation.

Directions

1. Choose a specific theme for exploration and formulate a key question. For example, as we are looking at the general theme of communication, you could ask each member of the group to write down the first four words that come to mind in response to the question: 'What are the most important things that are needed for effective communication between individuals or groups?' **2 min.**

2. Once every member has thought of four words, they should find a partner. The partners share their words with each other. The aim of this part of the exercise is to select a new combination of four words, ideally two from each partner's list. No new words are to be added. The partners are to look for what they have in common. If their words and ideas are very different, they should look for a compromise – they could, for example, decide on two words from each of their lists. In this way the pair will always emerge with a new combination of four words. **4 min.**

3. Each pair then joins with another pair, and the four work together to come up with a new combination of four words – the key words from their two lists. **6 min.**

4. The groups of four join up to make groups of eight and so on; the process continues until the whole group has synthesised one list of four words. If time is limited, the facilitator can call for the surviving words after about three rounds. These can be written up on the flipchart and everyone can be involved in negotiating to find the key words or to find ways of combining key concepts. **8 min.**

Feedback and discussion

Focus on how members felt about having to compromise their ideas. How difficult was it to reach agreements with others? Did this change as the groups increased in number? Do they think that this could provide a useful and positive method for group decision-making? Are they satisfied with the end result? **10 min.**

Notes

The exercise can be made more interesting by specifying that all words must have the same initial letter. This 'building' procedure can be used in difficult situations to find out what people think of, say, their youth club. It can be used to tease out the most important points for an agenda for a meeting. The exercise itself promotes debate.

Skills

Negotiation and compromise. Cooperation and understanding. Creative building on ideas.

Exercise 1.7 Back-to-back Listening

Time: 20 min.

Description

An exercise in pairs exploring the effect of body position in creative listening.

Aims

To explore creative listening. To see how the physical positions of listener and speaker influence the way they feel while communicating.

Directions

1. Ask participants to get into pairs and sit opposite each other. Each partner speaks for two minutes while the other listens. They might speak, for example, about someone they admire. There is no feedback or comment. **5 min.**

2. In the next round the chairs are arranged so that the speaker faces the back of the listener's head. On this occasion the topic might be something they really like doing. Each partner has a turn at speaking and listening. **5 min.**

3. For the final round the pair sit back to back with their heads touching. The topic might be a happy childhood memory. At the end of this round each partner should have spoken and listened three times. **5 min.**

Feedback and discussion

Which position felt best for the speaker? Why? Which position felt best for the listener? Why? What difficulties did the participants have in any of the three positions? In everyday life, do they ever feel as if they are talking to the back of someone's head? Discussion could focus on eye contact, difficulties with concentration and creative listening techniques. **5 min.**

Notes

It is possible to combine this exercise with any specific set of questions to explore a theme. You could also explore the effect of distance, getting the pair to move closer together and further apart, or set both partners speaking animatedly at the same time, so that neither can hear the other. The main aim of all this work is to get people thinking about the dynamics of communication.

Skills

Listening. Concentration. Expression.

Exercise 1.8 Countdown

Time: 20 min.

Description

A paired exercise to develop the skills of listening and summarising.

Aims

To experience speaking without being interrupted. To practise listening without interrupting. To practise the skills of summarising.

Directions

1. Participants should choose a partner and decide who will talk first. The first speaker will talk for three minutes on 'What I would do if I won the lottery' or another appropriate topic. Their partner will listen and not interrupt the speaker. **5 min.**

2. After 3 minutes call out time. The listener now has two minutes to feed back what they have heard the speaker say. **2 min.**

3. Call time after two minutes. The original speaker has one minute to comment on the feedback they have received. **1 min.**

4. Participants swap roles and repeat the exercise. **6 min.**

Feedback and discussion

Was it easy to speak for three minutes without being interrupted? As the speaker, what was the impact of having what you said summarised back to you? Was it easy to listen without interrupting? Did anything make it easier or harder to summarise what you heard? **6 min.**

Notes

We can ensure we have correctly heard what someone has said by checking our understanding of what has been said. We do this by summarising back to the speaker. The skill of summarising is developed further in Exercise 7.3, Facts and Feelings.

Skills

Listening. Summarising. Concentration. Expression.

Exercise 1.9 Attention Zones

Time: 35 min.

Description

A reflective paired exercise examining listening and practising listening with full attention on the speaker.

Aims

To identify different ways of listening. To examine how we listen in different situations. To practise listening with attention.

Directions

1. Give participants a copy of the handout on attention zones and talk them through the different zones.   **5 min.**

2. Ask participants to identify times recently when they have been in each of the different zones. Who were they with? What was the conversation about? Were they in the appropriate zone for that particular situation?   **5 min.**

3. Participants should get into pairs and share their reflections.   **5 min.**

4. Ask participants to identify a conflict they are willing to share with their partner. The conflict should be one that they care about but that is not too upsetting. Participants sit back to back. In pairs participants take it in turns to listen to each other's situation, trying to stay in Zone 1. Participants should make notes of when they slip into Zones 2 or 3.   **10 min.**

Feedback and discussion

What kinds of situations are appropriate for each of the different attention zones? How hard was it for participants to stay in Zone 1? What does this tell them? What would help to draw participants back to Zone 1 listening?   **10 min.**

Notes

Becoming aware of attention zones helps us develop our listening skills and make more conscious choices about how we listen to others. It can also help us be more aware of what might trigger us into Zone 2 or Zone 3 listening so that we can read the signs and return our focus to Zone 1.

Skills

Listening. Self-awareness.

Handout for Exercise 1.9

Attention Zones

There are three zones of attention according to Philip Burnard (1994), Emeritus Professor of Nursing at Cardiff University, who is an international author and lecturer on interpersonal skills and counselling:

In **Zone 1** your attention is on the person who is speaking, not on your internal dialogue.

In **Zone 2** your attention has moved from the speaker to your own reactions to what they have said. For example, if someone talks about a dispute with a particular person or profession you may start remembering when you had a similar problem. You start to listen for a pause so that you can interject.

In **Zone 3** your attention is no longer on the facts as the speaker is telling them, but on your fantasy of what you would do next, on the advice or information you want to give the speaker, or even on a pressing personal issue like buying a birthday card for a friend.

Exercise 1.10 What Language Do You Speak?

Time: 25 min.

Description

An individual and paired exercise looking at the way we use language and what it can tell us about ourselves.

Aims

To encourage awareness of the way we use and receive language, and of the differences in the way others use and receive language. To explore ways of communicating more effectively with those whose use of language differs from ours.

Directions

1. Participants are asked to think about a memorable incident from their childhood. In what way do they remember it? The visual or the emotional aspects? Or the smell or the physical feel of it? Participants note down which of these areas they find easiest to conjure up. When they are having difficulty trying to remember something, which part of the memory comes back first? **5 min.**

2. Individually, participants are invited to think about the language they use in dialogue with the people they are close to. Which of the following phrases would they use more easily: 'I'm out of touch' (tactile); 'I just don't see it' (visual); 'I don't hear your meaning' (aural); 'I can't get hold of it' (physical)? Individually, participants are invited to list familiar phrases under these headings: visual, physical, aural, tactile. They can add any others they think of. **5 min.**

3. In pairs they share their lists and any thoughts they have had during the exercise. What kind of language do they use? Are their closest friends the ones who use the same language? **5 min.**

Feedback and discussion

Invite participants to think about the people they have difficulty communicating with. Do they speak the same language? If not, how can they adapt in order to get through to them? Apart from spoken language, how do they best receive information – through the written word or through pictures? Or through any other means? What does this exercise tell participants about themselves? How can this exercise help us to develop our communication skills? **10 min.**

Notes

This exercise is useful for bringing up questions about how communication is affected by the differences in our use of language. Studying our own language can give us more self-awareness about how we process and communicate our experience of the world in relation to others. It can help us to understand why and when we get stuck in communication with others and identify the first subtle clues that we might be triggered into conflict.

It can also give us a greater understanding of the possible impact of what we say and provide us with clues to the concerns or needs of others. For example, by listening carefully and mirroring the way that someone speaks we may set them more at ease and thus aid the building of a more effective relationship.

Skills

Self-analysis and self-awareness. Recognition of personal communication habits and skills.

Exercise 1.11 Open and Closed

Time: 20 min.

Description

A physical group exercise exploring the concept of body language.

Aims

To explore 'open' and 'closed' body positions and how we use them in everyday interaction. To see how body language influences communication.

Directions

1. Ask each member of the group to think of an open shape for one of their hands and a closed shape for the other. These shapes are now shared with the whole group.   **2 min.**

2. Ask everyone to think of an open gesture and a closed gesture. These are now shared with the group. A short discussion could follow, looking closely at and analysing these positions. How do people feel when using them? When would they use them?   **3 min.**

3. Number the participants 1s, 2s or 3s. All the 1s will sit on the floor, all the 2s will sit in chairs and all the 3s will stand. In those positions they will each adopt an open shape and share it.   **3 min.**

4. Now ask everyone to change slowly from the open shape to a closed shape, all at the same time. You could then have the 1s start from the closed position, the 2s from the open position and the 3s from the closed position. It is interesting to see the two-way flow of movement from one to the other.   **3 min.**

5. A further development could be to put people in pairs. They could then respond to each other. A could close off, with B closing off as well in response; then A could open out, with B likewise opening out in response. Alternatively, A and B could respond to each other by adopting contradictory postures, with closure eliciting openness and vice versa. Ask participants to notice the effects.   **3 min.**

Feedback and discussion

How does body language influence our communication? Can we recognise situations where we have or use open or closed body positions? How does that affect the situation? Are there gender, racial or cultural differences in body language? How might they affect communication? **6 min.**

Notes

This is a good exercise for increasing awareness of how we use our bodies and how we read body language in others. An exploration of how body language varies from culture to culture would be valuable.

Skills

Physical awareness. Physical expression. Interpretation.

Exercise 1.12 Reading the Face

Time: 25 min.

Description

A paired exercise involving intense facial observation.

Aims

To encourage observation of subtle changes of facial expression and to relate them to emotions.

Directions

1. Participants think of three specific incidents in which they remember feeling exhilarated (such as going downhill fast on a bicycle), sad (such as an old friend moving away) and happy (such as hearing good news). Urge participants to avoid traumatic experiences when recalling something that saddened them. The exercise is not intended to be an ordeal. **3 min.**

2. Participants pair off and sit down opposite their partners. Each observes the other, in turn, silently recalling the three experiences. The person who is remembering should begin each recollection by telling their partner which experience it deals with (exhilarated, happy or sad) and end by announcing that they have finished. They should keep their eyes closed. The observer watches their partner's every facial movement. The facilitator could mention two or three of the following to give participants an idea of what they are looking out for: brows (furrowed, smooth, frowning); eyes (sideways movement); eyelids (fluttering, moving); nostrils (flaring, nose twitching); lips (any movement, curling, twitching, etc.); chin (wobbling); skin (tightening, slackening); breathing (change in pattern). Observers may note down their observations if they wish. **10 min.**

3. When each person has had a turn at recollection and observation, each goes back over the three experiences in a different sequence, again silently, while the observer watches to see if they can tell which experience it is. **5 min.**

Feedback and discussion

What observations did you make? What difficulties did you have? What did you find easy? What did you gain from the exercise? We constantly receive subtle messages from the faces of others and sometimes we are not aware of them, although we may be subconsciously affected. Likewise, what we are thinking and feeling is reflected in some way in our own facial expressions and gestures. **7 min.**

Notes

This is a useful exercise for building intimacy and trust within the group. Careful observation of this kind is an important skill for conflict resolution work and can enhance personal effectiveness in meetings. It is useful to be able to listen with eyes as well as ears.

Skills

Careful observation. Receiving subtle communication.

Chapter 2

The Spark

Immediate Responses and Coping Mechanisms

The raw material of fire lies still, but alive. Somewhere a live wire flashes, somewhere lightning strikes, somewhere there is friction. Sparks fly. Some fall on the earth and die. Some fall on damp wood and fade. Some fall on dry wood and live.

There are constant tensions, pressures and frustrations in our lives. Sometimes we rise to them and cope; sometimes they spark us off, and distress and tensions grow. Some people are more 'sparky' than others. They are the igniters of the fire, the hot-tempered initiators of conflict. We all react differently to different sparks; we all send different ones flying. Sometimes we are 'sparky', sometimes the opposite. Intervening in the development of the conflict at this stage is a job for the listener within us all. There is more opportunity for successful intervention before the fire really catches hold. Listening is a first step.

Focus

Sparks as the incidents, situations, reactions that ignite the fuel; degrees of combustibility; reacting and responding to conflict; using the self as a resource in conflict.

Key concepts

Personal combustibility; combustible situations; responding/reacting; developing new responses.

Key questions

How combustible are you? How combustible are those around you? How easily are sparks noticed? How do we respond to sparks or situations of tension? To what extent do you use your personal resources of voice, body, energy? To what extent can the use of these resources influence situations of conflict?

The Spark

Exercise 2.1 Fixed Positions

Time: 15 min.

Description

A quick group exercise to examine how our perspective influences our perception of a situation.

Aims

To examine the possibility that what we perceive depends on our perspective. To promote discussion on how our lack of knowledge or experience of a situation could influence our response to it.

Directions

1. Form a circle and ask one group member to stand in the middle. Remind participants to be respectful of this person. Their role is to stand still, facing the same way throughout the questions and answers. Ask someone standing in front of the person in the middle, 'How many eyes has the person in the middle got?' Ask someone standing behind the person in the middle the same question. Ask someone standing directly to the side of the person in the middle the same question. At all times participants must answer according to what they can actually see from their static position, not what they know is there. The answers will be two, none and one, respectively.   **5 min.**

2. You can then follow the same procedure with another member in the middle and choosing, say, the arms this time.   **5 min.**

Feedback and discussion

How does your perspective on a situation shape your understanding of it? How can we give ourselves a more complete picture more of the time? In what way can you relate this exercise to your everyday experiences?   **5 min.**

Notes

What happens if we get an opportunity to walk round the circle and perceive the person in the middle from all angles? It is a good idea to have a participant try it, and to ask them to give a running commentary on what they are seeing and how their vision of the person changes. The everyday analysis of this can also be developed in discussion. You could place a member at the other end of the room and ask them to walk slowly towards the rest of the group. How does distance influence what detail can be observed? How we perceive situations often informs our response to those situations. The beginning of a conflict can be based on an incomplete picture of a situation.

Skills

Observation. Self-awareness. Perception.

Exercise 2.2 Where Do You Stand?

Time: 20 min.

Description

A group exercise in which individual participants have to take a stand on a specific issue.

Aims

To determine the range of feelings within the group relating to various issues. To locate the areas of difference or the degree of consensus within the group.

Directions

1. Designate three areas of the room: one end is the 'Agree' position; the other end is the 'Disagree' position; a line in the middle of the room is the 'Not Sure' or 'Sitting on the Fence' position.

2. Read out the first statement: 'Violence is never acceptable.' Participants take up the position that reflects their response to the statement. Ask a number of volunteers to say why they have placed themselves where they have.   **5 min.**

3. Repeat the exercise by asking further questions such as: 'Adults should never lose their temper in front of children or young people' or 'You should back your mates no matter what', or design your own questions around a particular theme. You could also explore the first issue further (see the notes).   **5 min.**

Feedback and discussion

How easy was it to take a clear position of agreement or disagreement? Did they feel better in the outside positions or the middle position? Why was this? How did they feel about having to make up their mind so quickly? Did their ideas change when they heard other people's viewpoints? Were there any issues they felt they needed to know more about? How does this exercise relate to Exercise 2.1, Fixed Positions?   **10 min.**

Notes

This exercise can be useful for exploring one issue in depth. The three groups that emerge can work separately, exploring through discussion why they have chosen their specific position. They might be surprised to see how many different reasons and motivations emerge. Each group could then feed back all their different reasons to the other groups, perhaps using role-play or tableau presentation. The groups could then discuss their understanding of each other's positions. More time needs to be allocated for this.

Skills

Quick decision-making. Observation of the group. Being aware of one's own opinions and beliefs.

Exercise 2.3 Bombs and Shields

Time: 15 min.

Description

A whole-group exercise exploring the concept of bombs and shields in our lives.

Aims

To explore how others can act as the bombs and the shields in our lives. To consider who has the power in these situations.

Directions

1. The group stands in a circle. Everyone looks around and chooses someone from the group without telling anyone who that person is. This person is going to be their bomb. Now explain that as soon as you say 'Go' everyone must get as far away from their bomb as possible. **5 min.**

2. Ask everyone to choose another person in the circle again without telling anyone who that person is. This person is going to be their shield. When you say 'Go' everyone must get away from their bomb and try to position themselves so that their shield is between them and their bomb. At a certain point shout 'Freeze' and check where everyone is in relation to their bomb and their shield. If their shield is not between them and their bomb they are blown up. **5 min.**

Feedback and discussion

What did it feel like avoiding your bomb? What was it like trying to stay behind your shield? Who has the power in the situation: you, your bomb or your shield? Who controls where you move to? Who or what acts as a bomb or a shield in your life? Can you be your own bomb and shield? **5 min**

Notes

This exercise explores the different roles people can take in our lives. Often a person can be both a bomb and a shield. In this exercise the bomb and the shield have the power to make people move; in real life our bombs and shields can also determine our actions if we react to them without thinking or without making a clear and conscious choice to respond differently. This exercise is a lead-in to Exercise 2.4, Red Flags.

Skills

Inventiveness. Improvisation. Control.

Exercise 2.4 Red Flags

Time: 50 min.

Description

An exercise in pairs to explore triggers to conflict and our emotional reactions to them.

Aims

To understand what a conflict trigger is and identify personal conflict triggers. To explore language and situations to which we have strong emotional reactions.

Directions

1. Introduce the concept of red flags, or conflict triggers, using the analogy of a bullfight. Ask the group, 'Has anyone ever seen a Spanish bullfight?' Ask, 'Who is there?' Elicit the following responses: the bull, the matador and the crowd. Then ask, 'What happens?' Elicit the following responses: the matador waves his red cape at the bull, the bull sees red and charges at the matador, who sidesteps the bull. This happens again and again during which time the crowd cheers and the bull gets stabbed and eventually dies. Then ask, 'What makes the bull charge?' It is likely that participants will say the red colour of the matador's cape. However, bulls are colour blind. It is the movement of the cape that antagonises the bull. **5 min.**

2. Next, ask the following questions: 'When are you like the bull?', 'When are you in a situation where you feel your emotions are controlling you?', 'When might someone say or do something to you that has you metaphorically charge?' Remember not everyone reacts in the same way. Some people's reaction might be to get frightened or switch off. Ask for a couple of examples from the group. **5 min.**

3. The facilitators should demonstrate one of their own red flag situations by creating a very short role-play. At the start clarify where the scene is set and who the other person in the situation is. The role-play runs up to the moment the red flag is waved. Ask the group and then the participants what they thought the red flag was and what they thought might happen next. **5 min.**

4. Give each participant a copy of Handout 2.4, Red Flags, and ask them to fill it in. **5 min.**

5. In pairs, participants share as much or as little of their list as they want to. Each participant identifies a red flag situation to enact and with their partner creates a 30-second role-play. For example, if one participant has said that they feel angry when someone speaks over them, their partner should play a person speaking over them and the pair should act out the scence up to the point when the participant gets angry. **10 min.**

6. Invite as many pairs as time allows to share back to the large group and ask the group to guess what the red flag is and what emotion the person may be feeling. **10 min.**

Feedback and discussion

What was it like to show your red flag? What was it like to see others' red flags? Why might it be useful to know your own and others' red flags? How many red flags do participants have? Why is it important for people to know what they feel and think? Who controls their actions?

10 min.

Notes

Try to get a range of examples of emotional reactions to red flags as opposed to just anger. This will provide greater insight to the group. A more thorough analysis of conflict triggers can be accomplished by debriefing the role-plays; the following questions can be used: What is the red flag? What emotion do you feel when the red flag is waved? How strong is that feeling on a scale of 1 to 10? What sensations do you feel in your body? What is your first thought?

The debrief can be extended into a discussion of the immediacy of our reactions in conflict and the physicality of our thoughts and feelings in terms of how we experience them in our bodies. This is a useful insight in relation to working with young people.

This exercise leads into Exercise 2.5, Reaction versus Response.

Skills

Self-awareness. Role-play. Creative thinking.

Handout for Exercise 2.4

Red Flags

What people/things/situations anger me?	What people/things/situations frighten or upset me?
What sort of behaviours/words/gestures result in me switching off?	**What people/things/situations irritate me?**
What people/things/situations make me feel uneasy?	**What people/things/situations frustrate me?**

Exercise 2.5 Reaction versus Response

Time: 20 min.

Description

An exploration of the difference between a reaction and a response.

Aims

To examine the difference between a reaction and a response. To further develop the learning begun in Exercise 2.4, Red Flags. To explore the idea of 'choosing a response' rather than 'having a reaction'.

Directions

1.   Draw a line down the middle of a piece of flipchart paper. Write 'Reaction' as one column header and 'Response' as the other.

     Start with the Reaction column and lead a wordstorm using the following questions:

     ◦   What are some of the things you or others do when a red flag is waved?

     ◦   What is an 'action'? If we put 're' in front of it what does it mean?

     ◦   What characterises a reaction?

     ◦   How much time does a reaction take?

     ◦   How much thinking happens?

     ◦   How are you feeling when you have a reaction?

     ◦   How much choice do you have in that moment?

     ◦   How much power do you have – over yourself or the situation?

     Write up people's answers in the Reaction section.   **5 min.**

2.   With the Response column lead a wordstorm using the following questions:

     ◦   What were some of the outcomes people said they wanted in the Red Flags exercise (for example, to be treated with respect)?

     ◦   If that is what people say they want, is the reactive way of behaving likely to get it? For example, if you want to be respected but you shout or are offensive, are you like to get what you want?

     ◦   What characterises a response?

     ◦   How much time does it take?

     ◦   How much thinking happens?

     ◦   How are you feeling when you have a response?

     ◦   How much choice do you have in that moment?

     ◦   How much power do you have – over yourself or the situation?

     Write up people's answers in the Response section.   **5 min.**

At the end of Stages 1 and 2 your flipchart will look something like this:

Re/action	Response/Able to respond
Spontaneous	Considered
Automatic	Unfamiliar
Familiar	Takes time
Little time	More thinking
Little thinking	More choice
Little choice	More power
Little power	You control it
It controls you	Based on the outcome you want

Feedback and discussion

When are you in a state of reaction? When are you in a state of response? What are the physical and verbal signs that let you know that you are in one state or the other?   **10 min.**

Notes

You may say all or none of this as part of a process of enabling participants to understand the distinction between a reaction and a response. However, in order to create the distinction for others you will need to understand it for yourself.

Reactions don't take much time; they are quick. We're often not aware of our thoughts when we are reacting, although we may be very aware of our feelings, and our feelings are driving our actions. Reactions tend to be habitual – patterns of behaviour and thinking that we act out time and time again. Often we feel we don't have much control or power over our reactions. Clues that we are in reaction are when people use language like 'I can't' or 'They made me', or when people make statements implying that everyone else would do the same in their shoes. Our reactions can result in us ending up in uncomfortable situations, like an argument or a fight, a breakdown in communication or a relationship. However, there can also be a deep feeling of comfort in them. They are the culmination of habits of thinking and doing that we are very familiar with, and although we may not like the outcome, we are usually familiar with that too. We are always responsible for the ways we react to situations that 'make' us angry, whether the anger is sparked off by a deep-rooted conviction, old stories we have about ourselves or others or just a bad mood.

Responses will often take more time. They may involve us in challenging our own thoughts and opinions and searching for alternative ways of thinking and doing. They involve us in 'choosing' for ourselves. Making a response can involve us in recognising and acknowledging that we have strong feelings but not necessarily acting those feelings out. A way to think about response is that it is part of the word responsibilty – which we could take to mean an 'ability to respond'. Responding to a situation that we usually react to may involve us in trying out new behaviour and a new way of thinking. This can feel risky and uncomfortable as we are trying something new and unfamiliar. The first time we may not know the result it will create. If we don't get an outcome we like, we may feel drawn back to old patterns of behaviour which no longer serve us.

It may be important to mention that some reactions can be really useful, such as jumping out of the way of an oncoming bus. It is the understanding of the distinction and the awareness of reactions which are harmful that we are paying attention to in this exercise.

Sometimes this exercise can bring up feelings of blame/shame, right/wrong, good/bad. It is important to honour our habits even if they have been destructive or harmful. They are ways of coping that we learned or copied from our past and that have helped us to survive until now. Eventually new responses may become positive reactions.

Skills

Listening. Feedback. Making distinctions. Developing self-awareness. New thinking.

Exercise 2.6 Red Labels

Time: 40 min.

Description

An exercise that explores the labels we are given by others and those we give ourselves.

Aims

To explore the labels we are given or carry in society and how they determine our reactions in social situations. To begin to consider other effective and assertive ways of responding to those labels.

Directions

1. Wordstorm with participants all the different labels someone might be identified by in our society. Write them up on the flipchart. Ask participants to notice those that they have been given by others or that they identify with themselves. **5 min.**

2. Give each participant a copy of the handout and then ask them to fill it in for one aspect of their identity. **5 min.**

3. In pairs, participants share as much or as little of their list as they want to. Each identifies a red label situation to explore further and with their partner creates a 30-second role-play. For example, if a participant has said that they feel angry when someone labels them because of their religion, their partner should play that person telling them who or how they are because of their religion. The pair should act out the scene up to the point where the participant gets angry. **10 min.**

4. Ask as many pairs as you have time for to show back their examples to the large group and ask the others to guess what the red label is and what emotion the person is feeling. **10 min.**

Feedback and discussion

What does this exercise teach you about yourself? How much do the labels you haven't chosen determine your reactions? Do labels empower or limit you? **10 min.**

Notes

The shareback for this exercise can be deepened and extended using the questions suggested in the Notes section for Exercise 2.4, Red Flags. How we react in different situations is a function of who we are and how we think others perceive us. Looking at labels is a useful way of exploring this. How do you determine your responses – for example, as a pensioner, feminist, black person, immigrant, refugee, socialist, disabled person, taxpayer, religious person, person with HIV, businessperson? This exercise is developed further in Exercises 5.11, Defining Inappropriate Language, and 5.12, Challenge Carousel.

Skills

Personal recall. Self-awareness. Role-play. Creative thinking.

Handout for Exercise 2.6

Red Labels

As a .... (any label you have that others give you, or that you give yourself)

What's good about being a ....?	**What's difficult about being a ....?**
What angers me about being a ....?	**What frightens me?**
What frustrates me?	**What makes me switch off?**

Exercise 2.7 Immediate Responses

Time: 55 min

Description

An interactive exercise in pairs using prepared and improvised responses, leading to work on difficult personal situations.

Aims

To find effective responses to difficult situations. To explore ways of raising our status after a put-down. To find a good response to a situation we are likely to come up against.

Directions

1. Participants divide into small groups. This is an exercise in which everyone has a turn at being both the provoker (A) and the respondent (B), and at acting as an arbiter. Give each group a pile of the 'Strategy cards: phase 1', from Handout 1, on which are written various lines for A to say. **2 min.**

2. A and B face each other. A picks up a card and approaches B, saying the line on their card. As B has no idea what the card said they give their immediate response, with the aim of raising their bruised status. The remainder of the group act as arbiters and decide whether B's response was effective. If the arbiters consider that it was, the card is discarded; if not, the card returns to the pile for someone else to have a go at responding to it. **5 min.**

3. A and B return to their seats and the next two people take their places. Continue in this way either until all the cards have been used or until the time limit has been reached. **13 min.**

4. In the same groups, everyone is given a card on which is written a type of provocation – see 'Strategy cards: phase 2', from Handout 2. Individually everyone decides on a line appropriate to the brief, without telling anyone else what it is. The exercise goes on in the same way as before, but this time the provoker tells the respondent what their original brief was before saying the statement. **15 min.**

5. Participants divide into pairs. Ask each person to think of a provocative situation they face or are likely to be faced with soon. This is a chance for them to try out different responses with their partners. **10 min.**

6. Participants now share some of the successful responses from Stage 5 with the whole group. These could be recorded on the flipchart. **5 min.**

Feedback and discussion

How did people raise their status? What was an assertive response? How do they tend to react to provocative situations? How would they like to respond? **5 min.**

Notes

The second half of the exercise is an opportunity to rehearse strategies to deal with a difficult situation. It is important that individual needs are recognised and valued. The same solution or strategy will not necessarily suit everyone. If participants use put-downs or are rude in order to raise their status it is worth exploring what the long-term consequences of this might be, and whether a put-down that feels good in the short term really works for you in the long term. It would be a good idea to hear from the group about experiences and feelings they have had when on the receiving end of offensive remarks or comments. It is important to assist anyone who is upset by the work done in this exercise.

Skills

Quick responses. Creative thinking. Assertiveness. Creating strategies and problem-solving.

Handout 1 for Exercise 2.7

Immediate Responses

Strategy cards: phase 1

SHOP SECURITY STAFF Stop right there – what's in your pockets?	**TICKET COLLECTOR** Your ticket isn't valid for this journey.	**PARENT** Your sister is always really helpful when I ask her.
IN A QUEUE Can't you see there's a queue!	**IN A BAR** You'll have to leave – you're underage.	**FRIENDS** You didn't reply when I texted you.
IN A BAR You look lonely – do you mind if I join you?	**IN A SHOP** Cheer up love – it might never happen!	**OLDER PERSON ON A BUS** That seat's reserved for the elderly!
PARENT It's 2am and I told you to be in by 11!	**BORDER OFFICIAL** We need to check the contents of your bag.	**SOCIAL SETTING** Haven't I seen you somewhere before?

✓

Handout 2 for Exercise 2.7

Immediate Responses

Strategy cards: phase 2

BEING FORBIDDEN TO DO SOMETHING	BEING TOLD YOUR WORK IS NOT GOOD ENOUGH
A DECLARATION OF LOVE	AN ACCUSATION OF SHOPLIFTING
BEING LEFT OUT OF A GROUP OF FRIENDS	A FRIEND ACCUSING YOU OF ALWAYS BEING LATE

Exercise 2.8 Three to One

Time: 50 min.

Description

Interactive work in small groups looking at difficult situations.

Aims

To explore different responses to difficult situations. To recognise our current tactics and skills in handling such situations and to learn from the tactics and skills of others. To find appropriate responses to difficult situations.

Directions

1.   Ask participants to think of or write down an incident or situation they recently faced at work, at home or socially, which they feel they didn't deal with effectively.   **5 min.**

2.   Participants divide into small groups, and each group agrees on one person's situation they wish to work on. They explore what the following could be in relation to this situation: the most likely response; the most provocative response; and a 'successful' response (that is, the response which works for that person at that time – not necessarily a universally successful approach). The groups role-play their three options. If the most likely corresponds with the most provocative response, there will only be two options to enact.   **25 min.**

3.   Either join up as a whole group and watch some of the small groups role-play options, or join groups together in twos to show their options to each other.   **10 min.**

Feedback and discussion

What differences were made by the different approaches? What worked and why? What constitutes a successful response? In what ways was it familiar or unfamiliar? How often is the likely response the provocative one or the successful one? What skills or tactics are we already using to avoid the provocative response?   **10 min.**

Notes

The most likely response will often be an unsuccessful response. If the group feel, in their example, that the most likely response is the successful response, the facilitator could explore the factors that contribute to making the most likely response successful.

Skills

Clear thinking. Creative ideas. Improvisation. Finding strong points in ourselves and others.

Exercise 2.9 Slow Motion

Time: 15 min.

Description

An exercise involving individual, pair and whole-group physical work.

Aims

To develop physical control and balance. To develop concentration.

Directions

1. Ask everyone to stand in a circle with feet slightly apart and parallel, and with equal weight on both feet – a comfortable, poised position. Ask them slowly to take the weight off one foot and transfer it to the other, then ask them to reverse this process. As an observer you should hardly notice any movement.   **2 min.**

2. Ask participants to walk from their position in the large circle towards the centre of the circle, again transferring their weight from one foot to the other while this time moving very slowly forward. They should stop only when they have reached the centre of the circle or when their path is blocked by another participant.   **3 min.**

3. Everyone now walks normally round the room. On *freeze* everyone stops where they are. Are they standing in a strong, well-balanced position, knees slightly bent, weight evenly distributed, body – although still – not tense and stiff? Try pushing participants gently – from the front, side or behind – and see if they lose their balance. Partners can also do this in pairs, trying all the time to find the strongest and most stable position.   **2 min.**

4. In pairs, the participants stand opposite each other about six feet apart. Ask partners to move towards each other in slow motion, lifting their arms and moving to a position where they can shake hands. Again the movements should be as slow and as smooth as possible. There should be no talking in the room other than your occasional comments. If one pair finish early they should silently watch the others.   **3 min.**

5. Participants remain in pairs. Again in slow motion, one partner attempts to punch the other, who moves to defend themselves. No contact need take place. Like the handshake, this exercise relies on good balance and evenly distributed weight.   **2 min.**

6. You could end with a larger group or the whole group, participating in a slow-motion scene – a group fight or dancing, perhaps. You might need extra time for this.

Feedback and discussion

How important is it to have a feeling of control and balance in difficult situations? Did the work give any participants a feeling of confidence? What did it feel like moving slowly? What have they gained from the exercise?   **3 min.**

Notes

Practice in slow-motion work and freezing can be very useful later on when participants role-play potentially violent situations. Individual participants will need to exercise control and have confidence that others will do the same.

This exercise is also a physical introduction to the idea of balance: being non-defensive (that is, not going backwards) and non-aggressive (that is, not going forwards). It is very useful for achieving focus and control within a hyperactive group. Use the feedback questions throughout the exercise, not just at the end – participants may well need ongoing comments and encouragement. This exercise is further developed in Exercise 3.11, Attack and Avoid.

Skills

Balance. Coordination. Teamwork. Concentration.

Exercise 2.10 States of Tension

Time: 35 min.

Description

Individual, pair and group work exploring how situations are influenced by personal energy levels.

Aims

To explore the range of energy levels any individual can utilise, and how these levels can change the way people respond to us. To look at ways of using the energy we have and exploring levels that we find difficult to reach.

Directions

1.   Introduce the purpose of this exercise and describe the six different levels of tension:

    a.   *Sloth/collapse* A state of no energy, just about awake but unable to move or speak clearly.

    b.   *Laid back/very cool* Using the least energy possible for the situation: slow speech and movement.

    c.   *Everyday/one of the crowd* A 'normal' energy level: you wouldn't be noticed walking down the street – nothing unusual about you at all.

    d.   *Business-like/organised* Slightly unrelaxed, slight tension: going about a task that needs to be completed.

    e.   *Worry/tension* Unrelaxed and tense, slight panic creeping in: things are not going according to plan.

    f.   *Panic/hyperactivity* Growing into real panic – pulling out all the stops.   **5 min.**

2.   Ask each participant to explore for themselves what their idea of each level is. Using all the space, get the group to stand up and give them a specific task such as walking to the station to catch a train. Start from Level a and remind them of each level as you slowly take them through to Level f.   **10 min.**

3.   In groups of six, or as the whole group, depending on confidence levels, ask two volunteers to role-play to the rest. The group decides what level of tension each character is at and gives them a situation in which to interact, such as standing in a queue hoping to get tickets. During the role-play, the group can freeze the actors and change the tension levels, then unfreeze them and observe what effect the change has.   **5 min.**

4.   In groups of six, the participants are given a line on a card; for example, 'What do you think you are doing?' In turn they enter the space and say the line, each participant using a different energy level.   **10 min.**

Feedback and discussion

In Stage 4, how does the energy level affect how the statement is delivered and received? What effect could energy levels have on communication? When are certain levels more appropriate than others? Which energy levels do participants feel most familiar with? What is it like to experiment with a different energy level than the one you are used to? **5 min.**

Notes

Try to find out which levels people found easiest to use, and why they found certain levels difficult to reach or uncomfortable to use. Different people will have different ideas about each energy level and what it means to them. There are no right or wrong answers. The exercise is developed further in Exercise 2.12, Voice and Energy for Change.

Skills

Improvisation. Role-play. Control. Inventiveness. Concentration.

Exercise 2.11 Find Your Voice

Time: 25 min.

Description

An individual and paired exercise exploring tone of voice.

Aims

To explore the range of vocal tones that any individual can utilise. To examine how the use of the voice can affect how others respond to us, and how we feel in various situations.

Directions

1. Prepare in advance a card for each participant with a simple phrase written on each side. These will be short statements, commands and questions like 'I don't agree', 'Who is it?', 'Meet me later', 'What have you lost?'

2. Ask participants to form a circle. Each in turn says 'Oh, Henry!' in a different way. (There are apparently at least a hundred ways of saying it.)   **2 min.**

3. Give each participant a card. Each participant chooses one of the phrases from their card. Participants walk round the room individually, exploring their phrases in four different ways: certain/confident and loudly, certain/confident and softly, uncertain/unconfident and loudly, uncertain/unconfident and softly. Participants are likely to find that certain/confident and softly, and uncertain/unconfident and loudly are harder than their more common counterparts.   **4 min.**

4. Working in pairs, participants help to support and coach each other.   **4 min.**

5. Staying in the same pairs, ask participants to look at the second phrase on their card. They are going to experiment with that phrase, trying out different moods and emotions, again with both their soft and loud voices. Different ways of saying the phrase could include:

    Loudly: Assertive, aggressive, scared, commanding, excited

    Softly: Gentle, firm, scared, ashamed, supportive

    Ask one partner in each pair to nominate a mood, tone and volume, and the other to try saying their phrase in that way. They should then swap over.   **8 min.**

Feedback and discussion

What observations did participants make about the ways in which the sense of the phrase changed? What did participants find difficult? In what ways would they like to develop their voices further?   **7 min.**

Notes

This is a good exercise for assertiveness work. The exercise works best when the group are warmed-up and relaxed.

Skills

Concentration. Control. Imagination. Listening.

Exercise 2.12 Voice and Energy for Change

Time: 30 min.

Description

A small-group exercise to put into practice the work started in Exercises 2.10 and 2.11.

Aims

To consolidate previous work on voice and energy levels. To use both voice and energy together. To implement change within a role-play by adapting voice and energy.

Directions

1. Put the participants into groups of three or four and give out the phrase cards used in the last exercise. Each group has to find a way of combining their phrases to make a short scene that makes sense. They will need to decide who they are, where they are and what is happening. Ask them to think about how they are going to say their specific lines and what the energy level of their character is. **10 min.**

2. Each group should run through their scene. Now put two groups together so that they can share their work. The observer group should give feedback on whether the other group's scene was clear and audible, and on what they understood was being communicated. Then suggestions can be made as to which characters might make a change either to their tone of voice or to their energy level. The scene can then be replayed incorporating these suggestions. The observer group can assess how a change in one character affects the other characters – did they change too? How? The active group now becomes the observer group. **15 min.**

Feedback and discussion

Share the observations that were made in the different groups. How was change effected? How did it feel to make the changes? Did changes to a character mean that they progressed better or worse in the rerun? Did the changes to one character force the others to adapt? Did these changes take the others by surprise? Did you break a regular pattern of behaviour? How is this exercise relevant to real situations? **5 min.**

Notes

This exercise can open up a whole new range of possibilities for members of the group. It is the beginning of an exploration of how many choices we actually have. It is also a non-threatening look at making personal changes and examining personal habits. Later you may be exploring more sensitive or personal subjects and material, like violent and aggressive behaviour and change, and these exercises will help to prepare for this by building confidence in and awareness of effective communication.

Skills

Role-play. Imagination. Decision-making. Teamwork. Concentration.

Chapter 3
Smouldering
Powerlessness and Assertiveness

Sparks fly and land. A few catch. There is an indication of fire – slowly smoke begins to rise. The smell of smoke grows as the fuel begins to smoulder. The fuel is burning, but without strength. The smouldering coals lie still, ready either to ignite or to die down.

There is trouble brewing now. There is a rumbling of discontent, and the situation is being aggravated by persistent needling. The agitators enjoy themselves. They are rustling the coals to encourage the spark to catch. It is still possible to stamp out the fire at this stage if we recognise that it is there. Being assertive when feeling put down or oppressed, or when unfair demands are being made of you, is one way to prevent escalation of the conflict. When we rumble inside, or feel agitated and refuse to confront the causes of the conflict, we are refusing to admit to the warning signs of fire. We are, in fact, allowing ourselves to smoulder.

Focus

Short-term and long-term smouldering; the power of our thoughts; differences between personal and positional power; confronting and using power as a positive force; assertiveness as a way of responding to difficult situations.

Key concepts

Power – positional and personal; exploring the role of our thoughts in challenging situations; assertiveness – alternatives to 'attacking' and 'avoiding'; speaking for yourself – expressing feelings and needs; smouldering behaviour.

Key questions

How would you recognise smouldering behaviour? How do you smoulder? What are the differences between short-term and long-term smouldering? What is assertive behaviour? In what ways do you experience your own power and the power of others?

Smouldering

3.1	Sharing Power	35 min.
3.2	Statues of Power	25 min.
3.3	Positional versus Personal Power	30 min.
3.4	Hidden Thoughts	35 min.
3.5	Thought Patterns	50 min.
3.6	Describing a Habit	30 min.
3.7	Positive and Negative Thoughts	40 min.
3.8	You or I?	25 min.
3.9	'I' Statements	60 min.
3.10	Greet, Argue, Make Up	40 min.
3.11	Attack and Avoid	35 min.
3.12	Situations 1–5	55 min.

Exercise 3.1 Sharing Power

Time: 35 min.

Description

A paired listening exercise exploring the theme of power.

Aims

To broaden our understanding of power. To offer a forum in which participants can explore experiences of their own power and that of others. To practise creative listening.

Directions

1. Arrange the seating so that there are two concentric circles of chairs, the inner circle facing outwards and the outer circle facing inwards. There should be an equal number of chairs in the inner and the outer ring. Participants can now arrange themselves on the chairs. Everyone should be facing a partner. Introduce the exercise as a creative listening exercise.
    3 min.

2. Give participants two minutes each to talk to their partner on a given theme, then two minutes to listen to their partner talking on the same theme. The theme will be the first of the six situations listed at the end of the exercise. When the two minutes are up, ask the partners to swap roles.
    4 min.

3. All those in the inner circle now move round one chair to their right. Tell the group the second situation. Repeat the timed talking and listening process.
    4 min.

4. When each of the pair has spoken, all those in the outer circle should move one chair to the right and greet their new partner. The process continues: after each round the circles take it in turns to move to their right, and the situation changes.
    16 min.

Feedback and discussion

Participants might consider the following questions. How did it feel to be listened to with attention? How often do you give that attention to others? What does power mean to you? What negative power have you experienced or exerted? What is positive power, and how have you experienced or exerted it?
8 min.

Notes

This exercise focuses on the difference between power that is exerted over someone (negative power) and power from within (positive power), our personal strength which enables us to choose and control the direction of our lives. The exercise could also be used with another set of situations. It is a structured way of facilitating paired listening work and avoids the problem of constantly having to find new partners. The structure provides boundaries within which it is safe to talk about difficult subjects. You may want to speed up the exercise, either by cutting the time limit on each exchange or by reducing the number of situations.

Skills

Listening without expressing judgements. Listening with full attention. Verbal expression.

Situations

1 A time when someone had power over you and you were unable to do anything about it.

2 A time when you had power over someone else and used it badly.

3 A time when you had power and used it well.

4 A time when you felt scared but acted despite your fear.

5 A time when someone had power over you and you stood up to them.

6 A time when you felt hopeless, then suddenly knew what to do and did it.

Exercise 3.2 Statues of Power

Time: 25 min.

Description

A paired physical exercise using tableaux to explore the emotions we associate with power.

Aims

To look at the emotions we associate with power and how they affect us.

Directions

1. Divide the group into pairs. Each pair is going to produce two tableaux showing one person in a position of power and the other in a powerless position. Allow them a few minutes to prepare the tableau for the first person. Make sure they swap roles (so that the powerful figure becomes the powerless and vice versa) so they experience both perspectives. Then they should repeat the process to prepare the tableau for the second person.   **10 min.**

2. When they have prepared both tableaux, give each pair the opportunity to show them to the rest of the group. Ask for quick comments about what people observe. Ask each of the pair in each tableau to express what they are feeling in one word (for example, proud, scared, humble).   **10 min.**

Feedback and discussion

Which of the two positions felt more familiar to participants? Can they relate any of the emotions they felt to situations in their lives? What did they feel for the powerless person when they were in the powerful position, and vice versa?   **5 min.**

Notes

This exercise can quickly activate strong associations and emotions, and it is advisable to be conscious of this. Those who have strong emotional reactions might welcome an opportunity to talk about them, in which case it can be a good idea to have feedback in small groups.

Skills

Visualisation. Physical expression. Observation.

Exercise 3.3 Positional versus Personal Power

Time: 30 min.

Description

A structured role-play exercise in threes exploring the difference between power and status.

Aims

To explore the differences and similarities between personal and positional power, and between confidence and assertiveness.

Directions

1. Divide participants into groups of three. Ask each group to think of a clear line of positional power between three people, for example, from the chief executive to the secretary to the cleaner. On a scale of 1 to 10, the person at the top of the power structure is a 10, the person at the bottom a 1 and the third person somewhere in between.

    Agree a message to be passed from the top to the bottom and a response to be passed from the bottom to the top. For example, the chief executive tells the secretary to make sure the office is cleaned by the time work begins each day, and the secretary therefore tells the cleaner to get to work earlier; the cleaner makes a response to the secretary, who passes this on to the chief executive.

    Each group practises passing the messages down and up the line. When everyone is clear about their positional power, the second stage of the role-play can be introduced.
    10 min.

2. The line of positional power and the substance of the messages remain the same, but the characters' personal power, or assertiveness, is inversely proportionate to their positional power. The chief executive retains a positional power of 10 but assumes a personal power of 1 or 2; the cleaner still has a low positional power but takes on a personal power of 9 or 10. You can either give each group the numbers for their characters' personal power, or they can choose for themselves how they would like to alter the numbers.

    The scenes can now be played again, with the same characters and the same messages but the new hierarchy of personal power. If you are working with a group that enjoys drama, you might invite everyone to watch each group play the two versions of their scene. There can be great comedy in the contrast.
    10 min.

Feedback and discussion

What is the difference between positional and personal power? What characterises each? What differences do participants perceive when they are on the receiving end of each of these kinds of power? Can they identify aspects of both positional and personal power in the people they work with? How are they used?
10 min.

Notes

This exercise allows participants to try out different levels of personal power and to discover the effect that it can have on the course of events. It is encouraging to witness the fact that someone in a low position can assert themselves and thereby exercise a certain power of their own.

Skills

Role-play. Improvisation. Cooperation.

Exercise 3.4 Hidden Thoughts

Time: 35 min.

Description

A difficult communication exercise using role-play in groups of four.

Aims

To achieve close teamwork and communication. To explore the hidden thoughts behind what we say to each other. To practise intervening in thought patterns to bring about a positive resolution of a situation.

Directions

1. Set up a demonstration of the exercise first. Request four volunteers from the group. Ask for a typical conflict situation to work on; for example, between a manager and a member of staff where the manager is asking for a report that is overdue. The volunteers play the manager, the manager's thoughts, the staff member and the staff member's thoughts. Set the exercise up so that the two characters are opposite each other and the thoughts are behind their respective characters. **5 min.**

2. Begin the role-play. The voices can't speak unless their thoughts have spoken to them. So let's say that Staff Member's Thoughts (Thoughts 1) starts. Staff Member's Voice (Voice 1) will follow Thoughts 1, but with an opening statement that might not flow directly from the thoughts. For example:

    Thoughts 1: 'Oh, no! I hope she's not going to ask me for my quarterly report.'

    Voice 1: 'Hi Afshan, can we have a word about some time off?'

    Manager's Thoughts (Thoughts 2) has to reply before Manager's Voice (Voice 2) can begin:

    Thoughts 2: 'We just had a directive from head office about staff overtime – what did it say?'

    Voice 2: 'We've got a lot on at the moment, Steven, and you had last Thursday off.'

    The voices are listening to their own thoughts while at the same time listening to the other voice. The voices cannot respond to the other character's thoughts as this is impossible – we cannot hear the thoughts in someone else's head!

    In the given example, Voice 2 must accept her thought about the directive from head office, but she can choose either to express that thought directly or to cover it up. Either way the thought informs her. The conversation follows a set pattern:

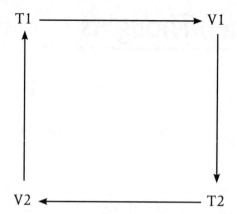

You may have to stop and start the role-play a few times to get it going well. **10 min.**

3.   When everybody understands the exercise, divide the participants into groups of five. Ask each group to choose a conflict situation that most people in their group can relate to. Then ask each group to appoint one person to observe which thoughts escalate the situation and which thoughts calm it down. Ask groups to role-play their situation as it would happen normally.   **10 min.**

Feedback and discussion

The focus of the discussion could be the relationship between what we say and what we think. When is it appropriate not to say what we're thinking? Can we tell when someone is concealing their thoughts? What are the kinds of thoughts that escalate conflict, and which thoughts help to find a resolution?   **10 min.**

Notes

This exercise needs plenty of preparation and you will need to give it time to develop. Ideally, participants should already have done all the various communication and listening exercises suggested in this section. The work on thoughts is developed in Exercises 3.5 Thought Patterns, 3.6, Describing a Habit, and 3.7, Positive and Negative Thoughts.

Skills

Concentration. Sensitivity. Judgement. Listening. Improvisation.

Exercise 3.5 Thought Patterns

Time: 50 min.

Description

An individual written exercise exploring patterns of thought at moments of particular stress or difficulty.

Aims

To identify recurring patterns of thought. To explore how these influence behaviour. To explore possible interventions in patterns that need to be changed.

Directions

1. Ensure the participants have a piece of A4 paper and a pen. Introduce the exercise by explaining the ideas outlined in the notes. **5 min.**

2. Ask each participant to think of a recent situation in which they felt angry or resentful and their reactions were not totally under control. The best situations to work with are those which are left unresolved, and in which the participant feels that their responses followed a familiar, habitual pattern. **3 min.**

3. Ask participants to divide their sheet of paper into three columns, headed (from left to right) 'Feelings', 'Thoughts' and 'Analysis'. The middle column should be widest. In this column they will write down every thought they had during the incident and number the thoughts as they occurred. (See the example that follows.) The aim here is simply to produce a record of their thoughts, without explanations, justifications or moral judgements. They should not record actions or emotions at this stage. Ask participants to write down the thoughts that they can readily recall – this is not a memory-testing exercise. **7 min.**

4. Ask participants to record their feelings at each stage in the left-hand column (see the example). **5 min.**

5. In the right-hand column, participants should record their analysis of what their thoughts were doing: for example, justifying feelings or actions; blaming; escalating the situation; calming the situation (see the example). **5 min.**

6. Ask one participant to volunteer their thought pattern for the group to look at and write it up on the flipchart. Go through it with the group, looking at how the thoughts and feelings relate to each other, where the feelings and justifications coincide, and what kind of interventions happened or could have happened. How did the participant try to stop the build-up of angry or resentful thoughts? How else could they have helped themselves? **10 min.**

7. Ask participants to look at their thought pattern and underline any points where they feel it would have been possible for them to react in a different way. What thoughts would have helped them to react differently? **5 min.**

Feedback and discussion

What did participants learn about themselves? How could this kind of exercise help them to deal with tough situations? **10 min.**

Notes

This exercise explores the thought patterns that lead people to behave in ways they are not happy with and which they feel they are not entirely in control of. It serves as an introduction to the exploration of the patterns of thinking and feeling that prevent us from changing the things we want to change. Such patterns often control our lives, but it is possible to intervene in our own psychological habits and regain control.

This exercise is a tester of how this can happen. It needs to be used daily if we want to break the thought habits of a lifetime. Individuals might find it useful to keep a daily journal of their thought patterns in 'high-risk' situations – that is, for instance, ones in which they feel angry, frustrated, withdrawn or aggressive. These ideas are developed further in Exercise 3.6, Describing a Habit, and Exercise 3.7, Positive and Negative Thoughts.

Skills

Analysis. Awareness.

Handout for Exercise 3.5

Thought Patterns

Example

Situation

Argument with a grumpy ticket collector who assumed that because I had lost my train ticket, I had tried to dodge the fare.

Feelings	Thoughts	Analysis
	1. This man is bloody grumpy.	
Annoyed	2. He could at least be civil to me.	
Indignant	3. How dare he think I've tried to dodge the fare.	Encouraging feeling of indignation
Angry	4. What's his problem? Why the hell is he so angry with me?	
	5. He's a grumpy old sod.	
Sympathetic, patronising	6. He's probably had a really bad day. He doesn't mean to be abusive.	Attempted intervention
Indignant	7. I don't care if he's had a terrible day. He's rude and he's jumping to conclusions and he has no right to take his anger out on me.	
Calm	8. Calm down, Sue. He's had a bad day and you're tired too.	Intervention
	9. Tell him you're sorry he's had a bad day.	
Rejected	10. Well he's bloody ungrateful and stupid to shout at me when I'm trying to be helpful.	Justification for shouting at him
Affronted, angry	11. Stupid idiot. He doesn't deserve any sympathy. He's an arsehole.	
	12. I want him to know I think he's an arsehole, 'cause he's a fucking grumpy mean old man and he's making me angry.	Passing blame to him – justifying my anger
Angry	13. I don't care how miserable he is. If I want to shout at him I will. He's made me angry.	
	14. Sod him – he deserves it.	Further justification for shouting
Uneasy, annoyed	15. I'm glad I shouted at him.	
	16. He's an idiot – he deserved it.	

Exercise 3.6 Describing a Habit

Time: 30 min.

Description

An exercise in which individuals define and confront a habit that they find difficult to change.

Aims

To understand the nature of our habits and determine ways of tackling them.

Directions

1. Participants can work individually or in pairs. Ask them all to identify a personal habit that they find extremely difficult to change, such as smoking, or eating unhealthily. **3 min.**

2. Ask participants to write down, or describe to their partners, an experience involving their habit – perhaps an occasion when the strength of the habit led them to behave antisocially or to break a rule. They should describe all the feelings they had as well as what they said and what they did.

    Ask them to list all their thoughts at the time, in the order in which they occurred, and number them from 1 to 10. Do they see a natural progression in these thoughts? Were they simply trying to rationalise (or justify) whatever action they were about to take? How did they go about this? **10 min.**

3. Are there any alternative thoughts they could have had? Ask participants to imagine what those alternative thoughts might be. It is important to recognise how our behaviour is supported by thought processes. If we can find ways of changing the thought process underlying a habit, then our behaviour might possibly change with it. **5 min.**

4. Participants should share some of their descriptions of their habits and the things they do to support them. **5 min.**

Feedback and discussion

Does targeting the habit in this way help us to understand our behaviour a little better? How can this understanding make it easier to work out possible strategies for change? Who is in control, the habit or you? **7 min.**

Notes

You can imagine applying this exercise to really tough subject matter: for example, using it with someone who is always getting into fights; with someone who habitually destroys relationships and friendships; with someone who finds it difficult to hold down a job; with someone who finds it impossible to control their anger.

In this exercise the individual does the work. There is no analyst – only the individual identifying their own behaviour, spotting trends and devising positive strategies for change. It is good, however, for members to help each other through this process. The sharing of information can be mutually informative.

Skills

Self-awareness. Clarity. Expression. Analysis.

Exercise 3.7 Positive and Negative Thoughts

Time: 40 min.

Description

An advanced communication exercise in groups of six, exploring how our thought patterns can undermine or empower us.

Aims

To explore how our thoughts can influence self-presentation and decision-making. To practise ways of working with both our confident and our doubting sides.

Directions

1. It would be a good idea to have already done Exercise 3.4, Hidden Thoughts, as many of the same skills and methods are involved. Groups of six are perfect for this exercise. Do not worry, however, if there are one or two participants left out – it is valuable to have observers who can give feedback.

2. Each group of six divides itself into two groups of three. In one group we have character A, with the two other members representing opposed elements of that character's personality. One plays A's positive and confident thoughts and feelings; the other plays A's negative and doubting thoughts and feelings. The second group divides in a similar way around character B. **5 min.**

3. Suggest a situation occurring between characters A and B. For example, A is the parent and B the child; A wants B to study harder for their exams. The two teams of three can prepare together. Each draws up a list of the strengths in the arguments of their character and their hopes, as well as the weak points and the fears of the character. **10 min.**

4. The procedure is as follows: Character A begins the dialogue but does not speak until the two assistants have fed them with thoughts (as in Exercise 3.4). Then B can reply, but only when their thoughts have been fed in. The two characters address each other all the time; the assistants are merely voices in their heads. The dialogue stops when A and B think they have come to a dead end, or when they have found a resolution. **15 min.**

Feedback and discussion

How have you coped in situations in which you have felt under internal pressure? Which aspect of your thought processes is dominant? Do these thought processes differ according to the situation? How can you take control of these thought processes? When do your thoughts lead you astray? When do your thoughts help you? What patterns can you recognise in your thought processes? **10 min.**

Notes

Before the group tackles an A–B dialogue, it is a good idea to do some preparatory work. For example, after the initial preparation described in Stage 3 above, the two teams of three could work separately for a while, trying to hold a conversation. The two thoughts would converse only with the character and not between themselves. The character would then reply to them. Group members could choose subjects that they are presently struggling with. Five minutes could be allocated for this.

The aim of the thoughts is to put pressure on the character. We then need to see how the character deals with these pressures coming from within. The group could work with a far more pressurised situation than the one suggested above. Once members are familiar with the format and techniques, they might, for example, explore a situation in which A is trying to persuade his old friend B to sell some drugs, and B is short of money but has just completed a prison sentence.

When members are comfortable with the exercise, the strict order suggested above could be eased up, with voices intervening at random. The group could also miss out the preparation stages and go straight into the situation. The situation would thus become totally improvised.

Skills

Teamwork. Judgement. Listening. Concentration. Clarity. Decision-making. Improvisation. Timing.

Exercise 3.8 You or I?

Time: 25 min.

Description

A warm-up group role-play exercise which explores the difference between 'you' language and 'I' language.

Aims

To understand the impact speaking in 'you' or 'I' language might have in conflict situations.

Directions

1. Ask participants to get into pairs facing each other in two lines across the room. Decide which line are As and which line are Bs. Set them up with a potential conflict situation; for example, A – you work night shifts and your neighbour B has a dog which barks all day whilst they are out at work. A – imagine you are about to knock on B's door and have a conversation with B about the dog.   **5 min.**

2. For the first role-play tell A that every sentence they say must start with 'You'. Let the role-play run for two minutes. Swap and replay the situation for a further two minutes so that each participant plays both roles.   **5 min.**

3. Ask participants to swap back and role-play the situation again; this time, however, they must avoid using 'you' language and instead talk about the situation using statements that start with 'I'.   **5 min.**

4. Draw a line down the middle of a piece of flipchart paper. Write 'You' as one column header and 'I' as the other and list the distinctions that participants have made in terms of feelings, thoughts and actions for each side when speaking or being spoken to in 'you' or 'I' language. Record any observations about the language used, tone of voice, volume of voice and body language, and the outcome.   **5 min.**

Feedback and discussion

What happened in the first role-play – did conflict escalate or de-escalate? What happened in the second role-play – did conflict escalate or de-escalate? What happened when you started using 'I'? How easy was it? How is it different from using 'you'? What do you most often use in a conflict situation?   **5 min.**

Notes

This is a fun, practical and useful warm-up which leads very effectively into Exercise 3.9, 'I' Statements. It begins to highlight the need to be aware of the language we use, our intention in any communication and the effect this might have in a conflict situation. It also shows that it is not only what we say but how we say it (tone, volume, body language) that affects the outcome.

Skills

Role-play. Listening. Improvisation.

Exercise 3.9 'I' Statements

Time: 60 min.

Description

An individual and paired exercise which provides a tool for expressing feelings and communicating assertively, effectively and constructively in conflict situations.

Aims

To understand and practise a tool for clear and clean communication in conflict. To show how it is possible to face someone with whom you have a problem without antagonising them or withdrawing from the problem. To practise making non-judgemental statements and using a structure that can open rather than close discussion of a difficulty.

Directions

1. Start by demonstrating what might happen if a situation is allowed to escalate using one of the facilitators' red flag situations (see Exercise 2.4, Red Flags). Ask participants to say what they see regarding language, tone of voice and body language, and the impact this has on the other person and the outcome; for example, both parties getting defensive, raised voices, blaming, pointing fingers, using 'you' language, not listening. **5 min.**

2. Introduce the structure of an 'I' statement using the handout. Explain that this is one way of speaking in a conflict situation which is intended to be clean (meaning free from judgement and blame) and clear (meaning specific and to the point). Highlight also that it focuses on your feelings and needs. You may explain that whilst it is not an instant solution to a problem, it is more likely to get a positive than a negative result. At its best it makes no demands, opens up possibilities rather than closing them down and leaves the next move for the other person. **10 min.**

3. Ask the group to support the trainer with the red flag situation to create a response using the 'I' statement model. Replay the scene using the 'I' statements only. Ask what that was like from the perspective of the speaker and the recipient. What difference, if any, did they notice? What did the rest of the group notice? **15 min.**

4. With participants in pairs, ask them each to develop an 'I' statement based on a 'red flag' situation or a current or recurring difficulty within their work. Partners can help each other to make their statements clean and clear. **10 min.**

5. Hear back two or three 'I' statements from the group, giving people an opportunity to comment on them and to offer suggestions as to how they might be improved. **10 min.**

Feedback and discussion

What is it like to use an 'I' statement? How easy or difficult is it? What kind of effect might an 'I' statement have? When might it be useful to use an 'I' statement – before, during or after a conflict? In what other ways could an 'I' statement be useful to participants? **10 min.**

Notes

This is a useful way of separating feelings and facts in order to clarify what a problem really is. The tool may feel stilted and unfamiliar, but with practice it can become an unconscious reaction rather than a laboured response. It may not work the first time you try it, but keep trying. It is a tough discipline and needs practice.

The exercise also highlights that it is not just what we say but how we say it that matters. Our body language and tone of voice may suggest a 'you' rather than an 'I' statement even if the words say otherwise. This is referred to as a disguised 'you' statement. Clear intention is an important ingredient in the successful use of an 'I' statement.

This model can also be a useful self-reflection tool even if you choose not to make a statement to the other person. We often don't think about what we feel or need in a conflict situation. This can provide the structure and space to do that and enable us to take responsibility for our part in a situation.

Groups as well as individuals can use the model to help them make a statement on something they feel strongly about. For example, a group of people with disabilities might approach a local bus company with the following statement: 'When we can't get on to local buses we feel angry and frustrated, because we need to have the same access to transport facilities as other people. Would you be willing to consider our needs when buses are designed?' It can be a good way for a group to focus their feelings and needs into a coherent statement for presentation to relevant authorities or audiences.

This exercise links well with Exercise 4.12, The Survival Game.

Skills

Separating feelings from facts. Clarity of expression. Sensitivity. Judgement.

Handout for Exercise 3.9

'I' Statements

An 'I' statement is a way of clearly expressing your point of view about a situation. It includes an expression of how the situation is affecting you and how you would like to see it change. The best 'I' statement is free of expectations and blame. It opens up a discussion and leaves the next move to the other person. Aim for your 'I' statement to be clear (that is, to the point) and clean (that is, free of blame and judgement).

Beware of 'you' statements which place the blame on someone else, hold them responsible, demand change from them or contain a threat. For example: 'When you deliberately clump around the house when everyone else is asleep, you are being defiant and disrespectful and you have got to stop it before things get really out of hand.'

'I' statement model

The action

> **'When…'** (if you say the facts of what happened, rather than your opinion, the other person may listen)

Make this phrase as brief, objective and specific as possible: 'When you arrange to meet me at a certain time and are late', rather than, 'When you mess me around'. The specific facts carry no blame and cannot be denied by the person to whom they refer.

My feelings

> **'I feel…'** (if you tell them your hurt feelings, rather than your angry feelings or what you feel like doing, you are more likely to be heard)

This describes how you feel. It should be worded in such a way that you are taking responsibility for your emotions and that it acknowledges the subjectivity of your emotions (for example, I feel irritated, annoyed, hurt, etc.). It is important that the description carries no blame, such as 'You make me so angry', or judgement, such as 'I feel you are uncaring and selfish.' Add a reason if it helps to clarify the situation for both of you: 'I feel hurt because I enjoy seeing you.'

My needs

> **'Because I need…'** (identify your needs rather than what you want the other person to do)

This stage acknowledges your needs and allows you to take responsibility for them in the situation. It involves sharing a personal reflection rather than demanding something from the other person. The need may be practical ('I need to know when and where we are meeting') or emotional ('I need to feel that my time is valued.')

Handout for Exercise 3.9 (continued)

My request

> **'Would you be willing to...?'** (a request rather than a demand, focusing on what you want the other person to do rather than what you want them to stop doing)

The final stage focuses on a request in order to obtain a desired outcome. It carries no expectation of change but clearly states how you would like things to be different and what you would like to happen rather than not happen: 'Would you be willing to arrange a time to meet which we are both able to make?'

Examples of clean 'I' statements

1. When fed up with others not washing up their coffee cups at the end of the day: 'When I arrive in the morning and see dirty coffee cups on the table I feel frustrated because I need a clean working environment. Would you be willing to organise a washing-up rota together?'

2. When feeling irritated about sharing a double desk with a colleague who isn't tidy: 'When your papers spread over to my side of the desk I feel cramped, because I need a clear space to work. Would you be willing to agree a separating line so that I know how much space I've got?'

3. Youth worker annoyed by club members taking drugs on the premises: 'When you break the rules, I feel anxious because I need to ensure the welfare of the club as a whole. Would you be willing to re-commit to keeping the rules?'

4. Youth worker to young people continually interrupting a girls' football session: 'When you walk into the room in a middle of a session I feel disappointed because I need to finish the work I want to do. Would you be willing to allow us to finish the session?'

5. Youth worker annoyed about having to run the club single-handed because a colleague arrives late: 'When I'm alone in the club at the start of the evening I feel anxious and uneasy, and I need to feel safe at work. Would you be willing to arrive on time or agree not to open the club until there are enough youth workers to cover it?'

Exercise 3.10 Greet, Argue, Make Up

Time: 40 min.

Description

An energetic group exercise to begin to explore habitual behaviour.

Aims

To begin to recognise the kinds of behaviour that are familiar to us and where we share similarities with others in the group.

Directions

1. Ask the participants to walk randomly around the room. Say stop and ask them to *greet* the next person they meet as if they were an old friend. Moving on, the next person they meet they will *argue* with. Moving on, the next person they meet they will *make up* with.
   3 min.

2. Run through this three times increasing and decreasing the speed, volume and energy.
   3 min.

3. Now ask the participants to gather in a large circle facing outwards. Explain that you are going to call out in turn 'Greet', 'Argue' and 'Make up' and that when you count to 3 you want everyone to turn around and go into a physical image of the word you have just called out.
   5 min.

4. For each word ask the participants to look around the room and 'find their family', that is, form a group with people whose words and/or gestures are similar to their own. Once together ask the group to create a frozen tableau to illustrate their interpretation and to give it a name.
   9 min.

5. Ask the participants to introduce their interpretations and notice the similarities and differences between the different images people have made.
   10 min.

Feedback and discussion

What are some of the verbal and body language clues you have seen in this exercise which warn us of an attitude or type of behaviour in ourselves or others?
10 min.

Notes

This is a great warm-up to Exercise 3.11, Attack and Avoid. It is best facilitated at a fast pace with a short debrief before leading straight into the individual work with handouts in Attack and Avoid. Because the exercise is very physical, it gets participants into their bodies and allows habitual behaviours to be experienced and revealed in a fun and inclusive way.

You could deepen the learning by asking the following questions: 'Do you recognise any of your habitual behaviours as aggressive or defensive, attacking or avoiding?' 'What is the usual outcome of acting in that way?' 'Is it possible to change the way we act in the moment?' 'How might this affect how we feel and what we then say?'

Skills

Vocal projection. Improvisation. Creative thinking. Self-awareness.

Exercise 3.11 Attack and Avoid

Time: 35 min.

Description

A group exercise introducing assertiveness and looking at aggressive and defensive behaviour.

Aims

To gain an understanding of what unassertive behaviour is. To recognise the kinds of behaviour that are familiar to us. To remind ourselves of verbal and body language clues which warn us of an attitude or type of behaviour in others. To notice these signs in ourselves and use them as an opportunity to recognise what kind of response we are likely to use and check that it is appropriate.

Directions

1. Ask participants to fill in the Attack and Avoid handout. How often do they find themselves responding in any of the ways listed on the sheet? **5 min.**

2. Show where the line is drawn between attacking and avoiding behaviour (between Revenge and Withdrawal) and ask everyone to note whether their behaviour is more frequently one or the other. Are their ticks concentrated in the upper half (attacking) or the lower half (avoiding)? **1 min.**

3. Wordstorm the words 'attack' and 'avoid', focusing on what they mean for the participants. Allow one minute for each word. Use a separate large sheet of paper for each of the two words. Use only half of the sheet at this stage, as you will need space later on. **2 min.**

4. You have determined what behaviour each word denotes. Ask individual participants to think of one personal reason why they would behave in each of those ways. Under the Why? heading record responses on the appropriate brainstorm sheet. (If you have a large group, you could take a sample.) **3 min.**

5. Ask individuals to consider how each of these behaviours would be expressed: what they would say, how they would say it and how they would express it physically. Under the How? heading record the responses. **3 min.**

6. Ask everyone to think of one word or phrase that they use when either avoiding or attacking, whichever is their most frequent behaviour. They should consider how it is said and the body language that accompanies it. An example of avoidance could be 'It doesn't matter', said in a way that indicates that it does matter and accompanied by shrugging the shoulders and turning the head away. **3 min.**

7. Ask somebody to give their word or phrase as a practical example. You might point out how the effect of what they say is very largely dependent on what they do, that is, their body language. With the 'It doesn't matter' example, you could suggest that they try using the phrase without shrugging their shoulders, and looking straight at the person they are speaking to. This will often have an effect on what they say and the message

communicated. In this example, the person may find that when they stop shrugging their shoulders and look straight ahead what they actually want to say is 'It does matter'.

5 min.

8.   In groups of three, get everyone to give their example while the other two in their group offer suggestions about how they might alter their body language to make their response an assertive rather than an attacking or avoiding one.   **7 min.**

Feedback and discussion

What signs can help us to recognise and even predict others' behaviour? What signs can we learn to recognise in ourselves that warn us that we are embarking on an unassertive approach? How can we alter our pattern of reacting and begin to learn a new response? How does it feel to change our body position?   **6 min.**

Notes

Assertiveness has as much to do with body language as with what we say. Conversely, what we say is often unconsciously influenced by our body language. If we adopt defensive physical postures, we are unlikely to speak assertively. On the other hand, if we adopt assertive body language, this can make it easier for us to speak assertively.

An assertive response is a centred response. We are balanced – not leaning forward in attack mode, not teetering backwards in avoiding mode. Although most of our confrontations are verbal rather than physical, there are often visual signs, even if they are tiny, of our body going on the attack or the defence. This exercise is a step towards using the signs we get and building up a desired response rather than an immediate reaction.

Skills

Quick thinking. Self-awareness. Investigation.

Handout for Exercise 3.11

Attack and Avoid

Behaviour	Rarely	Sometimes	Frequently
Nagging			
Shouting			
Interrupting			
Exploding			
Warning (If you can't do this!)			
Correcting (Look at the facts!)			
Persisting (I am right!)			
Insulting (You're pathetic!)			
Sarcasm			
Revenge (I'll get you back for this!)			
Withdrawal			
Sulking in silence			
Taking it out on the wrong person			
Declaring that you are being unfairly treated			
Talking behind someone's back			
Trying to forget about the problem			
Feeling ill			
Not wanting to hurt the other person			
Feeling low and depressed			
Being polite but feeling angry			

Exercise 3.12 Situations 1–5

Time: 55 min.

Description

An interactive group exercise exploring solutions for situations in which individuals find it difficult to be assertive.

Aims

To allow participants to create for themselves a picture of where their difficulties lie and determine a point at which assertiveness work could effectively begin. To explore what is needed for individuals to be assertive in their situations. To practise assertiveness skills.

Directions

1. Ask participants to divide a blank sheet of paper into five columns marked 1 to 5. Ask them to think of a situation at work where they have found it very difficult to be assertive – a situation that they would regard as a really tough problem. It could be either a one-off event or a recurring difficulty. They mark this down against number 5. Against number 1, ask them to write down something that they feel slightly uncomfortable about dealing with. Against 2, 3 and 4 they should write down other problematic situations, grading them from the minor difficulty of number 1 to the major dilemma of number 5. **5 min.**

2. In groups of three, each person shares one of their problems from lists 1 to 5. Encourage them to choose something nearer 1 than 5. To take on the hardest problem at this stage is not a good way to build up confidence and self-esteem. **5 min.**

3. Each group enacts each of the three situations as they happened or might happen. Everyone should be given the opportunity to work on their own situation. **15 min.**

4. The enacted scenes are shared with the whole group (or, if the whole group is large, with another group of three). Watch the first scene, then find out the priority and the desired outcome for the person involved (see the notes). Ask for suggestions from the observers as to how they could achieve the latter without abandoning the former. It is important that these suggestions are framed in a supportive way and are not judgemental or critical. Remind people to watch out for body language and other encoded messages, verbal as well as non-verbal. Once suggestions have been made, the scenes can be replayed all the way through with the altered, and we hope more assertive, behaviour. **20 min.**

Feedback and discussion

Participants might consider the following questions. What is your priority in each situation? What is your desired outcome? Can you achieve your desired outcome without compromising your priority? What will people take away with them from this exercise? What was useful to them? What advice or suggestions were helpful and why? What made it difficult and why? **10 min.**

Notes

An example might help to clarify the distinction between priority and desired outcome. A friend has given Sarah a birthday present she doesn't like. Her priority is not to hurt her friend's feelings. Her desired outcome is to take the present back and change it. If she feels she will hurt her friend's feelings in the process, she does not want to take the present back. Assertiveness in this instance does not mean taking the present back regardless. She must acknowledge her priorities and work with them, not against them. Is there any way in which she can achieve the desired outcome without sacrificing her priorities and without dishonesty?

Use the exercise to build confidence and practise using earlier voice or body language exploration to find an assertive response.

Skills

Clarity. Self-awareness and awareness of others. Improvisation. Assertiveness.

Chapter 4
Fanning the Flames
Anger, Enemies and Awareness

The smouldering coals lie still, ready either to ignite or to die down. Bellows blow, and the still coals flicker with life. The wind blows relentlessly, giving life to the fire. The flames lick, leap and grow. The fire has taken hold. There is no longer a possibility that it will fade.

The potential for conflict is about to be realised. There are provokers who will not let go, who will not let things lie. They push on, persist, irritate and inflame: they take the bellows and blow. Urging the fire to take is important for provokers. There are needs and hurts that will not die down or fade away. There is too much anger and hurt for some involved in the conflict to let go. They feel a need to maintain distrust and to nurture feelings of prejudice or hate. At this stage someone else could intervene and offer a forum for the expression of these difficult emotions. A conflagration can still be averted, but it is becoming increasingly difficult.

Focus

Expressing, receiving and containing anger; enemies and projection; developing new strategies for responding to anger.

Key concepts

What underlies anger: hurt, needs and fears; how we create enemies and opposition by projecting unacceptable aspects of ourselves onto others; facing our own anger and anger from others; developing skills for responding to anger.

Key questions

What lies at the root of our own anger? What lies at the root of the anger we receive from others? What do our 'enemies' and our scapegoats represent? How can we use our understanding to work with our own and others' anger?

Fanning the flames

4.1	Statements of Anger	25 min.
4.2	Emotion Pictures	15 min.
4.3	Statues of Anger	20 min.
4.4	Underlying Anger	35 min.
4.5	Yes/No	10 min.
4.6	Facing Anger	55 min.
4.7	Enemy Thinking	15 min.
4.8	My Enemy	30 min.
4.9	Personal Projection	20 min.
4.10	Facing Projection from Others	65 min.
4.11	Already Listening	30 min.
4.12	The Survival Game	75 min.

Exercise 4.1 Statements of Anger

Time: 25 min.

Description

An individual writing exercise looking at different ways of expressing anger and attitudes towards it.

Aims

To provoke thoughts about learned personal attitudes to anger. To recognise the messages about anger that we grew up with and to look at how they influence us.

Directions

1. Ask participants to think about their parents' attitude towards anger. (For 'parents', take the two most influential adults in their lives when they were growing up, for example, mother, father, guardian, grandparents, carers, teachers.) What did they hear them say about anger? How did their parents express their anger? What sums up their attitude? Get each participant to write a brief description (one or two sentences) of the point of view of one of their parents, for example: 'My mother didn't like anger. She thought it was an unnecessary display of emotion, and would rather not see it expressed.' If they can think of something actually said to them by that parent, they should write that down too, for example: 'My mother often said "I'm not angry, I want everyone to be happy. No one need be angry."' **8 min.**

2. Ask the participants to use the same idea but this time to apply it to themselves. What do you think about anger? What kinds of things do you say to people when you're angry? **4 min.**

3. Tell participants to join up with a partner and share as many of their statements as they want to. **8 min.**

Feedback and discussion

Can participants see either of their parents reflected in the way that they themselves express or repress anger? What do they value about what they were taught? Would they like to experience and express their own anger differently? In what way? **5 min.**

Notes

Anger can be experienced and expressed in many different ways. What we see and hear growing up has an enormous effect in shaping our understanding of it and how we feel able to express it. If time is short, Stage 2 of the exercise can be omitted. This exercise develops the work started in Exercise 1.4, Conflict Line-up.

Skills

Reflection. Expression. Self-awareness,

Exercise 4.2 Emotion Pictures

Time: 15 min.

Description

A group exercise using tableaux to explore feelings and reactions to emotions.

Aims

To gain an overall picture of what particular words mean to the group. For participants to express their immediate point of view without words.

Directions

Tell the group that you want to know what particular words mean to them. Emphasise that there is no right or wrong answer: you simply want to hear their personal understanding of the word. Ask the group to stand up. Ask them to give their immediate reactions, not their considered responses, to each word you give them. On hearing the word, each person should make an immediate physical picture, using face and body, showing what the word means to them. Use these words: anger, hate, frustration, love, anxiety. With each word, have participants hold the picture, and look around the room to find families of tableaux. For example, 'love' might produce some adoring pictures, some smothering, some sexual, etc. Participants can group themselves together with those who they feel have similar interpretations to their own. You will quickly have a visual impression of what the group feels about the subject.   **10 min.**

Feedback and discussion

Participants might consider the following questions. In what way does your experience of anger affect what the word means to you? What surprised you about what you learned of the reactions of the others? Were you surprised by your own reactions?   **5 min.**

Notes

Although we may speak the same language, our different experiences mean that we have different understandings of the same word. Using tableaux is an effective way of quickly seeing what a group thinks and feels about key words. For some it is easier to react physically to a word than to respond verbally. Use the feedback time to encourage the group to give their verbal reactions to the words and to explore their differences and similarities.

Skills

Instant reactions. Physical expression. Self-awareness.

Exercise 4.3 Statues of Anger

Time: 20 min.

Description

Paired tableau work on aspects of anger.

Aims

To make links between anger and hate, hurt and bitterness. To turn an understanding of an emotion into a visual expression. To raise ideas about both the creative and the destructive power of anger.

Directions

1. Prepare a set of index cards. On half of them write 'anger' on one side and 'hate' and 'aggression' on the other side. On the remaining cards write 'hurt' on one side and 'bitterness' and 'resentment' on the other. Divide the group into pairs. Each pair is given one card, so that half of the group will be working on anger and the other half on hurt. In each pair one person (A) moulds their partner (B) into a statue which expresses the key word. **5 min.**

2. B moulds A into a statue which expresses the words on the other side of the same card. (If B has been sculpted into an expression of hurt, their task will be to mould A into an expression of resentment or bitterness.) **5 min.**

3. Pick a few of the pairs of statues to comment on. Look at them as pairs, and encourage observation from the rest of the group. Which statue is expressing which emotion? Ask each statue how they are feeling in their chosen position. **5 min.**

Feedback and discussion

What connections do you make between hurt and bitterness? What connections do you make between anger and hate? In what ways do you see anger as a destructive emotion? In what ways might it be used positively? **5 min.**

Notes

Often when we are hurt we push away the pain in the hope that it will disappear. We may believe that it has gone, but it sometimes remains in the shape of bitterness or resentment. When anger is unacknowledged and has no outlet, it can turn into aggression or hate. Accumulated anger and hurt, when they finally break out, can be very destructive. But anger itself need not be destructive. You can use this exercise to open up the discussion on anger as a positive force.

Skills

Visualisation. Interpretation. Observation.

Exercise 4.4 Underlying Anger

Time: 35 min.

Description

A physical and written exercise about what underlies an instance of anger.

Aims

To encourage participants to consider and express what lies beneath an instance of personal anger.

Directions

1. Draw a picture of an iceberg on the flipchart. Ask participants to identify what you have drawn. If they cannot guess, tell them. Ask them what they know about icebergs. Elicit that about 90 per cent of an iceberg is under the water and therefore not visible. This exercise explores what is behind the emotion of anger. Wordstorm some of the ways people express anger. **5 min.**

2. Ask everyone to write down (in one sentence) a situation at work where they felt really angry. For example: 'I felt angry when my contribution in a meeting was ignored.' **2 min.**

3. Explain that a layer of hurt very often underlies anger. Ask everyone to write a sentence about the hurt behind their anger in the situation they thought of. For example: 'I felt hurt because it seemed that nobody valued my opinion.' **2 min.**

4. The reason for the hurt is often an unmet need. Ask everyone to write a sentence describing their needs in the same situation. For example: 'I need to be accepted and valued by my colleagues.' Needs can be practical or emotional. **2 min.**

5. Alongside the need are often fears. Ask participants to think about what fears might lie behind their anger and write a sentence about them. For example: 'I have a fear that I won't be able to win my colleagues' respect.' Fears can be rational or irrational. **2 min.**

6. Participants turn to a partner and share their sentences with them. If anyone has had difficulty with the exercise, their partner can help them unravel their feelings. **6 min.**

7. Ask for volunteers to share their sentences with the whole group. This can be useful if anyone is struggling to identify the underlying feelings. It is important that each layer relates to the layer above it and focuses on the needs and fears at the time. **5 min.**

8. If you have time choose one person's situation to explore further. Ask for four volunteers. The person whose situation it is sculpts each volunteer into an image of one of the feelings; for example, one person represents the *anger*, one the *hurt*, one the *need*, etc. Line up the images one behind the other in front of the rest of the group. The person whose situation it is reads out their sentences, with each of the images peeling away to reveal the image underneath. This can be a powerful way of representing the strength of the feelings underneath. **5 min.**

Feedback and discussion

What is the value of understanding the feelings that underlie an instance of anger? In what ways could it help you in your work? What do you notice about your fears in relation to the instance of anger?   **6 min.**

Notes

Anger and hurt are often two sides of the same coin. It is an important step in facing the anger of others to know what lies beneath our own anger. This exercise is a way of discovering some of the hurt, needs and fears underlying a personal experience of anger. If we can identify the fears that lie at the roots of anger (either our own or others), we can begin addressing those fears rather than remaining caught up in the outward emotion. Often the fear that underlies an instance of anger, once identified and expressed, can seem out of proportion to the actual instance of anger, but fear is often the driver for anger. The tableau technique used in Step 8 is known as a tableau peel by Leap trainers and is a useful way of demonstrating the power of our feelings. This exercise is developed further in Exercise 4.6, Facing Anger.

Skills

Uncovering, clarifying and expressing feelings.

Handout for Exercise 4.4

Underlying Anger

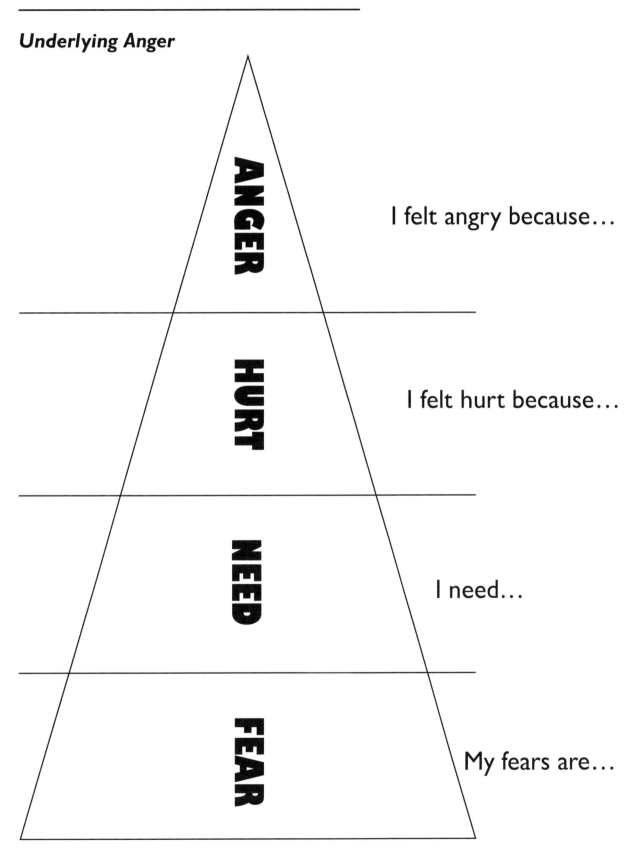

ANGER — I felt angry because…

HURT — I felt hurt because…

NEED — I need…

FEAR — My fears are…

Exercise 4.5 Yes/No

Time: 10 min.

Description

A physical warm-up exercise exploring experiences of resisting and insisting.

Aims

To remind ourselves of our experiences of resisting and insisting. To prepare for the next exercise.

Directions

1. Draw an imaginary line down the centre of the room. Participants sit on the floor in pairs back to back over the line with their arms linked. Designate one side of the line as the Yes side and the other as the No side. The Yes side needs to gain ground, the No side to defend it. When you say 'Go' participants push against each other to try and gain or defend ground. The only words they can use are yes and no, according to which side they are on. Swap around so that each side has equal time being Yes and being No.   **3 min.**

2. In the same pairs, standing up and facing each other, participants argue, using only the words yes and no. Again each person should try being both Yes and No.   **4 min.**

Feedback and discussion

Ask the following questions. What did it feel like when you were winning or losing? What was your most effective strategy: shouting, speaking firmly, withdrawing? Think about the strategies you use in your life when you are up against what seems to be a hopeless situation. Do they get you the results you want?   **3 min.**

Notes

In the course of this exercise, participants might find themselves recalling (and perhaps drawing inspiration from) specific incidents in which they have played either the yes or the no part. They should hold on to those memories as reminders of the areas in which they need to work on their assertiveness. The exercise can reveal patterns in participants' ability to say Yes or No. The work could be developed to explore situations in which participants have particular difficulty and to help them rehearse ways of saying what they want to say.

Skills

Focus. Quick responses. Imagination. Concentration.

Exercise 4.6 Facing Anger

Time: 55 min.

Description

A small-group exercise putting into further practice the ideas and techniques explored in Exercise 4.4, Underlying Anger.

Aims

To practise receiving someone's anger and helping them transform it into constructive action. To practise planning a strategy before taking action. To practise observing a partner's performance and giving constructive feedback. To practise receiving constructive feedback.

Directions

1. This first stage is to prepare the ground for the rest of the exercise. Ask participants to think of a time when someone unleashed their anger on them. What was said? How were they approached? How did they respond? What do they think their hurts, needs and fears were? **10 min.**

2. Ask participants to share this remembered situation with a partner. They will then assume the role of the person who unleashed their anger on them. The partner will attempt to locate this character's hurts, needs and fears. Then they swap over and repeat. They should compare notes at the end and see if their thoughts about the hurts, needs and fears of the angry character were alike. **10 min.**

3. Divide participants into groups of four and subdivide this group into two teams. The first team should have Anger and an adviser; the second team should have Receiver and an adviser. Both teams are given a card with a dispute written on it. (The two cards should be the same.) An example could be: 'You always thought that you received the same pay as other colleagues. You have recently discovered that this is not so and you feel very angry.' The angry team decides the identity of the individual that they will approach in order to focus their anger.

    The teams now prepare separately. The angry team prepares its opening line while the receiving team, anticipating some of the feelings that might emerge, prepares some possible opening responses which might get behind the anger. **10 min.**

4. Anger and Receiver now begin the role-play. Anger starts. Receiver attempts all the time to get behind the anger and to influence the discussion constructively. The two advisers observe closely and monitor how their partners are doing. Everyone could now swap roles and play the situation again, but extra time might need to be allocated for this. **10 min.**

5. In their pairs, the participants look at all the techniques and responses that emerged from the role-play. When the pairs have finished, the four can share their comments and observations. **5 min.**

Feedback and discussion

How did the participants feel about their in-role performances? What did they learn by participating and observing? How did the feedback from the observers help the participants to understand what had occurred? Were the teams well prepared, and how much did they have to deviate from their original planning?   **10 min.**

Notes

You could explore the nature of observation. What were the advisers looking for and why? It is useful to get them to articulate their approach and see in what way it could be improved. This exercise could also be used for the development of evaluation and self-evaluation skills.

Skills

Role-play and improvisation. Listening and observation. Clear feedback. Responding under pressure.

Exercise 4.7 Enemy Thinking

Time: 15 min.

Description

A wordstorm to gather ideas and perceptions of what 'enemy' means to the group.

Aims

To gather information about the range of opinions and perceptions within the group without discussion or argument. To establish a starting point for work on enemies and 'enemy thinking'.

Directions

1. Wordstorm the word 'enemy'. Ask the group what it means to them. What were they taught to think an enemy is? Who were they taught to see as the enemy? What feelings do they associate with the word? What fears do they associate with it? Record all the answers on the flipchart. **5 min.**

2. Introduce the idea of 'enemy thinking', for example: 'The enemy are wrong', 'We're better than them', 'They want to hurt us', etc. How do participants think about their enemies? How do we make enemies? **5 min.**

Feedback and discussion

What does 'enemy thinking' and having enemies do to us as a society and individually? What are the similarities and differences in our understandings of what 'enemy' means to us? What do our enemies have in common? **5 min.**

Notes

This is a brief idea-gathering exercise to encourage participants to see the scope of the work you will be doing on enemies. It is primarily a stimulation exercise to raise questions, not to answer any. Encourage participants to make one-word and short-phrase contributions to the wordstorm so that they do not get bogged down trying to explain and justify what they are saying.

Skills

Quick thinking. Free association. Group acceptance of ideas.

Exercise 4.8 My Enemy

Time: 30 min

Description

A paired tableau exercise exploring the concept of 'enemy'.

Aims

To examine our enemies. To find links between our enemies and us. To explore threats represented to each by the other.

Directions

1.   Ask all participants to write down three things that they hate or fear about their enemy. They should try to think of someone or a group of people they really dislike, either for themselves or for what they represent. If they find it impossible to think in those terms, they can use as an enemy a person or a group of people they were taught to hate or fear as a child.   **5 min.**

2.   Put participants into pairs. One partner starts by shaping or sculpting the other into a statue of their enemy. For example, A sculpts B into a statue of a large man in an arrogant pose, smoking a cigar.   **5 min.**

3.   B now responds by shaping A into a statue that represents how the statue B might see A. For example, B (as a large man with a cigar) might sculpt A into an ungrateful woman who doesn't know when she's got a good deal. Ask A and B how they feel as a large man with a cigar and an ungrateful woman. What do they gain from this part of the exercise?   **5 min.**

4.   Examine a selection of the statues within the group, as pairs. Each completed picture shows us A and B as enemies. We see what they think of each other. Ask each of them, in character, to complete the sentence: 'You are my enemy because…'.   **5 min.**

5.   Everyone watching looks for common characteristics in the two statues. What is at the root of their hatred? What threatens them? What do they fear in one another? For example: A is threatened by B's positional power and fears his lack of respect; B is threatened by A's personal power and fears what she represents.   **5 min.**

6.   If you want to change round and give B a chance to sculpt A into their enemy extra time might be needed.

Feedback and discussion

What do we and our enemies have in common? What fears do we share? What threats do we represent to each other?   **5 min.**

Notes

Carl Jung, the influential psychologist, suggested that we project what we dislike or fear about ourselves onto others and dissociate ourselves from it, thereby creating enemies. It is a tough concept to apply to ourselves because it requires us to see ways in which we and our enemies are the same. The idea is explored further in Exercise 4.9, Personal Projection. A good starting point is to look at what we have in common on a practical level, such as families, lifestyle, expectations, dreams, children.

Skills

Visualisation. Physical expression. Observation.

Exercise 4.9 Personal Projection

Time: 20 min.

Description

Individual work with paired feedback, looking at links between our enemies and ourselves.

Aims

To recognise aspects of ourselves that we often do not accept. To explore links between what we do not accept in ourselves and what our enemies represent.

Directions

1. Ask participants to draw up a list of things they dislike about themselves. Ask them to find things that they are genuinely uncomfortable with or would really rather not acknowledge. They then add to the list things that they feel they are not, and would like to be. This list will not be shared with the whole group. **5 min.**

2. In pairs, partners look at their lists alongside the lists they made previously (in Exercise 4.8, My Enemy), stating three things they dislike about their enemy. Ask them to see how many links they can make between the two lists. What do their enemies have in common with themselves? Can they see in them anything they reject in themselves, or anything they would like to be and are not? Make sure that each pair spends time on the lists of both partners – five minutes each. **10 min.**

Feedback and discussion

What links did participants find between what they do not accept about themselves and what their enemies represent? What does this tell them? **5 min.**

Notes

Understanding how we project ourselves onto others can help us to confront our own fears and hates, and can be of value in facing projection thrown at us from others. Projection is a defence mechanism whereby we 'project' our own undesirable thoughts, motivations, desires and feelings onto someone else. It is a common process that everyone uses to some degree.

Skills

Self-awareness. Empathy.

Exercise 4.10 Facing Projection from Others

Time: 65 min.

Description

Paired role-play exercise focused on facing anger and projection from others.

Aims

To explore what underlies expressions of hatred and bigotry. To develop strategies for facing anger and projection from others with greater confidence.

Directions

1. Ask participants to think of examples of times when they or someone they know has faced anger and projection from others. Examples for this may already have been highlighted by the work in Exercises 2.6, Red Labels, 4.7, Enemy Thinking, 4.8, My Enemy and 4.9, Personal Projection and could include facing projection based on race, gender, religion, sexuality, disability or economic status. Give each person an index card and ask them to write down an example of the type of projection they wish to face. **5 min.**

2. Put participants in pairs and ask them to decide who is A and who is B. B gives their card to A, whose role is to take on the point of view expressed on the card. A begins a conversation with B along those lines. B listens to what A has to say, and tries to find out what needs and fears lie at the root of it. A should take on the point of view with all their imagination, using every argument they have ever heard and trying to get into the shoes of someone who really does hold that view. B should listen carefully, questioning and probing, and try to identify the real problem underlying what A is saying. **10 min.**

3. Feedback in pairs: did A feel that B was reaching something close to the truth? What questions were most revealing? What tactics were effective? How did each feel in their role? **10 min.**

4. Pairs join up to form groups of four. Ask each group to draw up a set of guidelines (similar to the handout at the end of this exercise) for use when facing someone else's projection, in the form of bigotry, prejudice, hate or aggression. What does the individual on the receiving end want to achieve? How do they react? What do they say? It will help participants to use their experience of Stage 1, concentrating on how successful the questioning process was and which tactics and approaches had effect. **15 min.**

5. Each group now chooses one of their four earlier examples of projection to work on again. Two members of the group take on the point of view from that example. The other two work together, following their guidelines, to try to get to the root of the comments. Allow five minutes for preparation, five minutes for the role-play and five minutes for feedback within the groups. **15 min.**

Feedback and discussion

What guidelines could you use in your working environment? How could they influence your work? How can we find out whether the anger we are feeling towards someone includes projection? What guidelines could we employ in order to check ourselves? **10 min.**

Notes

The sharing and feedback is important, and can give participants practical ideas to take away with them. It is important to find out if any participants found the contentious points of view upsetting. Their feelings can be shared with the group. In this way awareness of these issues is heightened. This exercise is developed further in Exercise 5.12, Challenge Carousel.

Skills

Active listening. Drawing out information. Empathy. Patience.

Handout for Exercise 4.1

Facing Projection from Others

Guidelines on facing hate, aggression or projection

1 Allow the anger and emotion to come out. Don't try to arrest it.

2 Listen carefully. Feed back what you are hearing and how you interpret it. For example: 'It seems to me that you're angry about the idea that black people get better housing than you.' This process could be developed into an exploration of the protagonist's insecurities, needs and fears.

3 Remember that reasoned argument will reach unhearing ears. When someone is very upset or distressed, they will not be able to listen. Factual information or other points of view will not be heard until the roots of the anger are addressed.

4 Acknowledge your own boundaries to yourself, such as how much insulting language you can take. Once you have established that you are not going to preach, you might be able to state what is acceptable and unacceptable to you without being felt to be judgemental.

5 Offer personal disclosure if and when appropriate, allowing the other individual to see you as a fallible human being with your own needs and fears.

6 Your personal safety is always paramount

Exercise 4.11 Already Listening

Time: 30 min.

Description

A small-group exercise to introduce the concept of 'already listening'.

Aims

To introduce the concept of 'already listening' or background listening. To consider its influence on how we approach challenging situations.

Directions

1. Ask the group for their first thoughts about young people by asking them to complete the sentence 'Young people are…' Record their answers on the flipchart. Ask them not to censor or modify their thoughts but to say them out loud.   **5 min.**

2. Ask them their responses to the list of words on the flipchart. How would their thinking affect how they approach young people in a work context; what would their thinking have them be or not be, do or not do? Explain that the term 'already listening', or background listening, describes the stories we are already telling ourselves in our heads about a new situation which are based on past experiences.   **5 min.**

3. Put the participants in groups of four or five. In each group one person needs to identify a challenging situation they are facing or would like to revisit from the past. In their groups, they will consider the key attitudes they are already bringing with them that will impact on this situation:

    What is their 'already listening' about?

      ◦ the other person (They are…)
      ◦ the challenging situation (This is…)
      ◦ yourself (I am…)
      ◦ the context in which the situation will happen (for example, the home, work, street) (It is…).   **10 min.**

Feedback and discussion

What did participants notice about their 'already listening'? How is it useful to identify key attitudes before dealing with a challenging situation? How can you utilise this learning to identify realistic aims in a challenging situation?   **10 min.**

Notes

Here we will be using 'already listening' as a tool to inform us of where we are starting from in any given situation. Thinking through our 'already listening' can help to uncover any feelings, concerns, fears or questions about a challenging situation. By increasing our awareness it can inform our approach to this situation and help us develop new, more constructive responses. Exercise 4.12, The Survival Game, develops this concept and demonstrates how if we change our thoughts we may also be able to change our behaviour and thus the outcome of a situation.

Skills

Self-reflection. Cooperation. Analysis.

Exercise 4.12 The Survival Game

Time: 75 min.

Description

An individual and interactive exercise exploring how our interpretations of past events influence our behaviour in the present.

Aims

To distinguish between the facts of an event and the interpretation of it. To identify some of the reasons why people have different interpretations of the same event. To explore the empowering effect of revising our personal interpretations of past events.

Directions

1. Ask for a volunteer and ask them to sit still in front of the group with their head resting in their hands. Pointing to the volunteer ask the group 'What's happening?' Write up their answers on a flipchart. Keep asking the question until the flipchart is full.
    5 min.

2. Ask people to identify which of the words or phrases on the flipchart are facts, that is, what is indisputable and real. Circle each of the facts on the flipchart. Ask the group, 'What is a fact?' Ask the participants to check the facts against the still image in front of them; for example, if someone insists that it is a fact that the person is thinking, ask them how they know the person is thinking. If someone says that the person has their head in their hands, ask them to break this statement down into the actual facts – their hands are around their face, their head is between the fingers of their hands, and so on. **10 min.**

3. Ask the group, 'If the words circled on the flipchart are facts, what label can you give to the rest of the words?' Explain that they are their interpretations or their stories. The aim is to get the group to question the difference between a fact and an interpretation. Human beings have been making stories, interpretations and assumptions about facts for as long as they have existed; human beings are story-makers. Ask the group what we base our actions on: the facts or our interpretations? There is nothing wrong with creating stories apart from when the decisions we make based on our stories entail a personal cost. Thank the volunteer with a round of applause and move on to the next part of the exercise.
    5 min.

4. Ask each participant to think of a situation where they made an interpretation that resulted in them taking an action that cost them something in some way. For example, a friend cancels a meeting at short notice; my interpretation is that the friend doesn't really value my friendship. I am standoffish with my friend the next time they phone; the friend feels rejected and there is a rift in our friendship. Participants get into small groups. Each participant creates four tableau pictures of the facts, their interpretation, the decision they made and the consequences of that decision for themselves, by sculpting the other members of their group.
    15 min.

5.   Ask one volunteer from each group to share their pictures with the large group, giving a one-line description of each tableau. Ask the rest of the group to provide some alternative interpretations of the facts that would open up more possibilities and choices for the volunteer. With the example above, alternative interpretations may be that the friend is very busy with work or that they have something important going on in their personal life. Experiment with looking at how different interpretations might change the decision and thus the consequences. **20 min.**

6.   In the same small groups, participants address the following questions: When working with young people, is there any kind of situation that you habitually interpret in a certain way? What kind of conversation does this situation set off in your head? What 'conversation' could you have instead which would open up other possibilities for the situation? (For example, whenever a student asks me to explain something again, I have a conversation in my head that tells me that they couldn't be bothered to listen the first time. An alternative conversation might be one that tells me that they are keen and conscientious and want to learn.) Changing that conversation in my head will totally change the way I respond to the situation in question. The aim is to create a 'new listening' and with it an inner voice that offers possibility rather than limitation. **10 min.**

Feedback and discussion

How can participants use what they have learnt about themselves? How can this help them to deal with tough situations? How can they develop what they have learnt outside the session or workshop? How can it support them in their work with young people? **10 min.**

Notes

This exercise is based on ideas about the way we interpret what happens to us and what we see around us. The first premise is that each of us is a survival machine and the instinct to survive affects our emotional as well as our physical well-being. The second premise is that when we feel hurt, disrespected or unloved the survival instinct leaps to our defence and helps us interpret whatever happened in a way that will protect us from further hurt.

When these things happen we have a conversation in our heads that pushes us in a particular direction. This conversation will sometimes help us to justify our interpretations and sometimes to question them. These conversations are inspired by our outlook on life, so someone with low self-confidence may have a recurring conversation around themes such as 'They don't really think I'm any good' and 'I won't be so stupid as to be taken in by them', even when they are being praised or valued. This kind of conversation will protect someone against further hurt, but it will also prevent them from seeing things from a different perspective; indeed, it might prevent them from seeing the truth.

We all have our own ways of interpreting what happens to us, just as we all have habitual thought patterns (see Exercise 3.5, Thought Patterns). These habits of interpretation can be formed by accumulated incidents or by one vital event. For example, a young person who is never given any encouragement by their parents may at some point make a decision about what that means: 'They don't care, no one cares.' The interpretation might bring with it a defensive resolve: 'I'm going to make sure I won't get hurt again.' So the young person's interpretation of their parents' behaviour becomes a pair of glasses through which they view everything that happens to them. Any support or encouragement offered will have to get through the conversation in the head which is saying, 'They don't mean it. They're only trying to break you down. Don't let them get to you.'

People who have thought patterns that lead consistently to violent or abusive behaviour are probably looking at the world through a pair of heavily tinted glasses and listening to a loud conversation in their head which backs up their vision of things. We all, however, view the world through our own interpretive glasses.

This work is well worth doing with young people but needs a safe environment with secure boundaries. Questioning our interpretations of the world, and of our own lives, is an immense challenge and should not be undertaken without suitable supportive structures.

It is important to make a distinction between what we do and do not have power over. We may not be able to change where we were born, or who our family is or what has happened to us – our circumstances – but we can change what they mean to us and, therefore, how they will influence our future.

Skills

Awareness. Analysis. Physical expression.

Handout for Exercise 4.12

The Survival Game

Experiment with seeing how different interpretations might change the decision and thus the consequences.

Example 1

Fact	A friend cancels a meeting at short notice.
My interpretation	The friend does not really value my friendship.
Decision	I am offhand with my friend next time they phone.
Outcome	The friend is upset and a rift opens up in our friendship.

Alternative interpretations	The friend is very busy with work. They have something important going on in their life which they didn't want to reveal in a phone call or by text.
Decision	
Outcome	

Example 2

Fact	A student asks me to explain something again.
My interpretation	The student can't be bothered to listen to me.
Decision	I am impatient and dismissive of the student.
Outcome	The student loses enthusiasm and motivation.

Alternative interpretations	The student is keen and wants to learn. My explanations are not clear. The student may need extra help.
Decision	
Outcome	

Handout for Exercise 4.12 (continued)

Example 3

Fact	A young person is uncommunicative in a groupwork session.
My interpretation	The young person is not interested in the session and is trying to wind me up.
Decision	I try to include the young person whilst not addressing the issue directly with them.
Outcome	The session continues but the atmosphere in the session is uncomfortable for all.

Alternative interpretations	The young person is upset about something unconnected with the session.
	The young person is feeling unsafe in the session for some reason.
Decision	
Outcome	

Chapter 5

Stoking the Fire
Inequalities and Empowerment

The flames have taken hold. They are burning with energy. The fuel is consumed as the flames grow higher. The stokers add fuel to the fire. It demands to be fed. The fuel burns quickly. The fire catches on huge logs and takes hold with speed. Attempts to put the fire out meet with little success. The logs refuse to be extinguished, and there are many more ready to burn.

The conflict is fuelled by arsonists, who delight in the fury of the flames. They are the stokers. The fuel is within their reach. The logs that are added to the fire are large and weighty. They are the logs of prejudice and oppression and will not easily crumble or disintegrate. They cast shadows over our lives just as they stoke our fires. They burn with vigour and resist efforts to put them out.

There is still time for someone to enter the conflict and work on strategies for resolving it. But their work will be tough. They will needs a strategy not just to put out the near-blazing fire, but to bring about long-lasting change. Social structures that engender injustice do not just disappear.

Focus

Identity and prejudice; oppression and injustice; challenging oppression; empowerment; power relationships.

Key concepts

Identity and prejudice; oppression; patterns of behaviour; empowerment.

Key questions

How does our place in society shape our identity and perception of ourselves? How does prejudice lead to injustice and oppression? What tools do we need to challenge oppression? What tools do we need to enable young people to challenge oppression?

Stoking the Fire

Exercise 5.1 Pam, Reggie and Vernon

Time: 30 min.

Description

Exploration in small groups of the behaviours shown by persecutor, victim and rescuer.

Aims

To explore the type of behaviour that maintains unequal power relationships. To identify personal experiences of the roles within a 'power game'.

Directions

1.	Go through Handout 2: The Power Game Triangle with the group.	**9 min.**

2. Divide the participants into small groups and give each group one of the three profile cards (see Handout 1). Ask them to fill out their card, giving two items under each heading. The idea is to build a caricature of each of the roles: persecutor, victim and rescuer. **5 min.**

3. Each group chooses one of their phrases, a tone of voice and a body stance to go with it. In the case of Pam Persecutor, for example, the phrase might be 'Don't ever speak to me like that again'; the tone of voice might be loud and sharp; and the stance might be standing up and pointing a finger. Each group practises enacting their character. They should aim to present their character to the other groups by speaking and acting in unison. Rather than exploring individual interpretations of the voice, the group should work to find a collective identity using the agreed phrase, tone of voice and body stance. **3 min.**

4. The groups now present themselves to each other in role. Maintaining their group identity as either persecutor, victim or rescuer, the groups move around the room exploring the ways in which they interact with each other. At this point the groups may want to use different phrases or even develop a conversation. If there are more than three groups you will get the opportunity to see what happens when, for example, two victim groups meet. **8 min.**

Feedback and discussion

How did participants feel in the roles they were playing? Which of the roles is most familiar to them? Can they think of current situations in which they themselves are playing one of these roles? Who else do they know who habitually plays one of these roles? **5 min.**

Notes

We use the terms 'persecutor', 'rescuer' and 'victim' to signify roles, not people. There will be aspects of each role that we are familiar with, either in ourselves or in others. In conversation an individual could shift from one role to another or play aspects of all three. The maintenance of this particular power triangle, however, relies on the participation of all three roles.

Each of the roles has its own payoffs, which is why participation in the triangle continues. When we use the word 'victim' we mean the role, not someone who is a genuine victim of oppression. A genuine victim needs real support and help, and will welcome possibilities of change. On the other hand, those who are in the victim role typically reject possible change; for example, they might respond to every possibility offered, 'Yes, but...'

This exercise is an introduction to Exercise 5.2, The Power Game, which follows.

Skills

Physical expression. Observation. Exploration.

Handout 1 for Exercise 5.1

Pam, Reggie and Vernon

Profile cards

Pam/Pete Persecutor

Typical phrases:

Tone of voice:

How she/he sits, stands, walks:

Reggie/Regina Rescuer

Typical phrases:

Tone of voice:

How she/he sits, stands, walks:

Vera/Vernon Victim

Typical phrases:

Tone of voice:

How she/he sits, stands, walks:

Handout 2 for Exercise 5.1

Pam, Reggie and Vernon

The Power Game Triangle

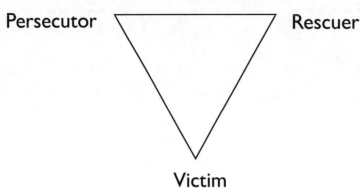

Persecutor · Rescuer · Victim

Persecutor *Bully*

Says: *You won't… You mustn't… You will… You must… It's your fault.* Uses imperatives and orders. Language full of blame and threat. Presumes that the victim is always wrong and needs to be corrected.

Payoff: Often get what they want in the short term.

Drawbacks: No basis for respect from others. Often unsatisfactory relationships with people.

Needs within the role: To feel important and powerful. To be in control.

Rescuer *Do-gooder*

Says: *You can't… Poor you… You shouldn't have to… You need my help.* Uses placatory words. Language full of put-downs towards the victim and admonitions towards the persecutor. Presumes that the victim is inadequate and incapable of self-help.

Pay-offs: Manipulative power and control.

Drawbacks: Insecurity of falling between two camps. Often afraid of losing friends.

Needs within the role: To be liked by everyone. To be indispensable to the lives of others.

Victim *Doormat*

Says: *I can't… I'll fail… I don't know how… It's my fault.* Uses negatives and denials. Language full of dismissals and self-pity. Assumes inability to succeed or change.

Pay-offs: Others take responsibility. No high expectations to live up to.

Drawbacks: Low self-esteem. Powerlessness.

Needs within the role: For others to take responsibility for them.

The Power Game Triangle is from Karpman (1968).

Exercise 5.2 The Power Game

Time: 50 min.

Description

A role-play exercise in threes looking at the power dynamics in relationships.

Aims

To explore the behaviour of the persecutor, the victim and the rescuer. To explore our own feelings when playing each of those roles. To look at ways of changing the roles.

Directions

1. Ask participants to spend a few minutes individually thinking of a time when they have been in the persecutor role, the rescuer role and the victim role. What did their behaviour involve? What kind of language did they use? Refer to all observations made in Exercise 5.1, Pam, Reggie and Vernon. **5 min.**

2. In groups of three, ask participants to decide on an imaginary situation for the exercise. For example, a family might be engaged in an argument about where to go on holiday, or a parent, a child and the child's teacher might be discussing the child's progress. Each person can play either an adult or a child but there must be at least one of each in each group. Each participant keeps their character throughout the exercise. Each character will experience the three different roles in the power game. **5 min.**

3. Ask participants to draw an imaginary triangle on the floor which corresponds to the power game triangle (see Handout 2 for Exercise 5.1, The Power Game Triangle). One person stands in each position. Begin the first round. Participants play their characters in the role of persecutor, rescuer or victim, according to their position on the triangle. Allow three minutes only. **3 min.**

4. Allow one minute for participants to jot down their feelings and thoughts about their role. **1 min.**

5. Each participant moves round one place on the triangle and therefore changes the role they are playing. Everyone, however, keeps their character. Someone playing a parent and a persecutor in the first round would therefore maintain the character of the parent but would now take on the role of the rescuer. Participants should move round the triangle physically so that they actually walk towards their next role. Participants continue the discussion in their new roles, again for three minutes. **3 min.**

6. Again, allow one minute for participants to jot down their feelings and thoughts about their role. **1 min.**

7. Participants move on to the next position exactly as before, keeping their character but changing their role, and continue the discussion for a further three minutes. **3 min.**

8. Again, allow one minute for reflection on the new role. **1 min.**

9. Share the Handout for Exercise 5.2, The Triangle of Change. Discuss how the roles differ from those in the power game. How might the interaction between the characters change? **10 min.**

10. In the same groups of three, with the same characters, again take up positions on the triangle. This time the role of the rescuer is replaced by that of the responsive, whose aim is to help the victim and the persecutor move out of their roles and move towards finding a resolution. Spend ten minutes with one person in the role of the responsive. The task of those playing the persecutor and the victim is, with the help of the responsive, to move out of their fixed roles and towards resolution. **10 min.**

11. Allow two minutes for the participants to note down any differences experienced as a result of the one changed role. (We recommend that extra time be allowed if all three are to take on the role of the responsive. Twelve minutes will be sufficient time for only one person to take on this role.) **2 min.**

Feedback and discussion

What were the possibilities of changing the power dynamics in the role-play? Did they recognise any aspects of their own behaviour in any of the roles they played? Which roles do they habitually play with which people and in which situations? What have they gained from this exercise? **6 min.**

Notes

Often in a power game, it is only one player who decides to change the situation. That individual can transform the whole game. Just as the rescuer can become responsive, so the persecutor or the victim can put themselves in a position where they can see the dispute as an opportunity for both teaching and learning. When such change occurs, you no longer have people interfering and instructing each other; you have people interacting. It is no longer a power game.

This work could focus on individual experiences of being in one of the three power game roles and what it would take to transform it, that is, what verbal language, gestures and body language could turn the role into something more constructive.

Though opposed in certain obvious ways, victim and persecutor can have much in common. Victims do not like being victims and may turn on a rescuer, blaming them for not having done something well enough and thus placing themselves in the persecutor position and making the rescuer a victim. For example:

Young person (victim): What am I going to do? I've got no money and I was sacked from my job last week.

Youth worker (rescuer): I'll ring up your ex-employers and see what I can do. (Ex-employers will not change their decision.)

Young person (persecutor): Sod you. Think you can help, but you don't do a thing. You're useless.

Skills

Improvisation. Role-play. Interaction. Expression.

Handout for Exercise 5.2

The Power Game

The Triangle of Change

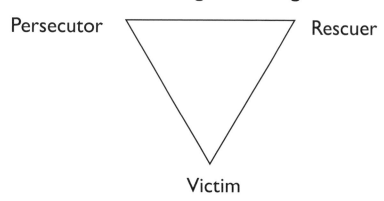

Potent

Behaviour: Demonstrating good leadership, listening to the needs of others, looking for potential and possibilities, solution-focused.

Key skills: Self-leadership, solution-focused, calm and patient with others, questioning, drawing out underlying needs, taking responsibility for self.

Responsive

Behaviour: Listening to the feelings and needs of others, reflecting and responding rather than reacting, asking questions and helping to identify underlying issues.

Key Skills: Active listening, staying impartial, encouraging responsibility, reflecting back to others, drawing out feelings and needs, calm and patient with others.

Vulnerable

Behaviour: Able to experience and share difficult feelings and needs without expecting others to find solutions. Open to hearing other viewpoints and to change.

Key skills: Identifying and articulating feelings and needs, both one's own and others, open to possibilities and solutions, able to take responsibility for one's own behaviour.

Exercise 5.3 Assumptions Quiz

Time: 25 min.

Description

A quick paired exercise exploring assumptions made about the training team.

Aims

To explore assumptions group members may have made about the training team. To highlight the ease with which people make assumptions. To introduce a discussion about assumptions and stereotypes.

Directions

1.   This exercise requires advance preparation. Find eight facts about yourself and your co-trainer that are different and, if possible, that go against stereotypes. Examples could include: where you were born; your nationality or heritage; your education levels; your family make-up or marital status; your class background; your age. List these facts on a flipchart.

2.   Divide participants into pairs. Tell them you will give them eight statements, each of which is true for one or other of the training team. As each statement is read out, the pairs need to decide which trainer it is true for and why, and note down their answers. Keep the statements covered up and reveal them one at a time.   **8 min.**

3.   At the end, work through the statements, asking each pair who they thought it was about and why, before giving them the answer.   **8 min.**

Feedback and discussion

Why do we make assumptions about people? What do we base those assumptions on? What are the disadvantages of making assumptions? What does it feel like to be on the receiving end of assumptions? What would be preferable to that and why?

Try to draw out what the stereotypical assumptions would be (if the group has not picked them). Part of the reason for including this exercise is to encourage participants to start talking about these issues.   **9 min.**

Notes

This exercise works best when the participants do not know the trainers very well. If it is run when participants know quite a lot about the training team, you may wish to use public figures instead of yourselves. You may need to name the possible assumptions as participants may be concerned about voicing them. Assumptions are often an unsophisticated way of assessing how safe (physically or emotionally) we feel with that person but they can often be based on stereotypes and prejudice. Stereotyping is holding a generalised view of a group of people which is generally negative. It means seeing someone as having the characteristics of a group rather than seeing them as an individual. Prejudice is a pre-judgement or preconception about a person, often based on little or no information. Many of our stereotypes and prejudices are absorbed from the world around us, and we may not be aware that we hold them.

Skills

Self-awareness and group awareness. Expression. Observation. Analysis.

Exercise 5.4 Identity Shields

Time: 35 min.

Description

An individual and paired exercise in which participants explore and share aspects of their identity.

Aims

To explore what particular aspects of identity mean to participants. To identify the components of identity. To examine how our identity is shaped by others.

Directions

1. Prepare in advance a copy of the Diversity Wheel (see p.131) on a piece of flipchart paper.

2. Each participant needs a piece of flipchart paper and a wide choice of coloured pens to use. Ask participants to draw a shield of any shape and divide it into four sections headed Race, Nationality, Religion and Culture. Participants should draw a picture in each section which represents what each of these concepts means to them personally. Explain that they can use diagrams, pictures, symbols or drawings but that they should avoid using words. Ask them to write a personal motto which encapsulates their philosophy or approach to life. **10 min.**

3. Participants divide into pairs. Each individual shares their motto and shield with their partner, asking questions and looking for areas of similarity and difference. **5 min.**

4. Remind participants that there are other aspects of identity, such as sexuality, ability or disability, age and class. Ask the pairs to discuss the following questions:

    ◦ Which aspects of their identity are visible?

    ◦ Which are invisible?

    ◦ Which aspects did they choose?

    ◦ Which are not a choice for them?

    ◦ Which were chosen for them?

    ◦ Which would they choose if they could? Why?

    ◦ Which aspects of their identity are most important to them? Why?

    ◦ Which have they changed or modified to fit in?

    ◦ What is the gain and cost of changing? **10 min.**

Feedback and discussion

Refer to the Handout for Exercise 5.4, The Diversity Wheel. What did participants learn about their identity doing this exercise? What aspects of their identity have they explored? Why? What aspects of their identity are more/less important to them? Why? What contributes to feeling that they belong? What contributes to feeling that they do not belong? Who decides their identity? **10 min.**

Notes

The aim of this exercise is to engage participants in exploring aspects of their identity. People tend to claim or reject specific identities based on society's acceptance or rejection of that group. People may therefore identify more positively with some aspects of their identity and feel guilt or shame about other aspects. We may change some aspects of ourselves in order to survive or to fit into society.

Skills

Self-awareness. Interpretation. Listening. Sensitivity.

Handout for Exercise 5.4

Identity Shields

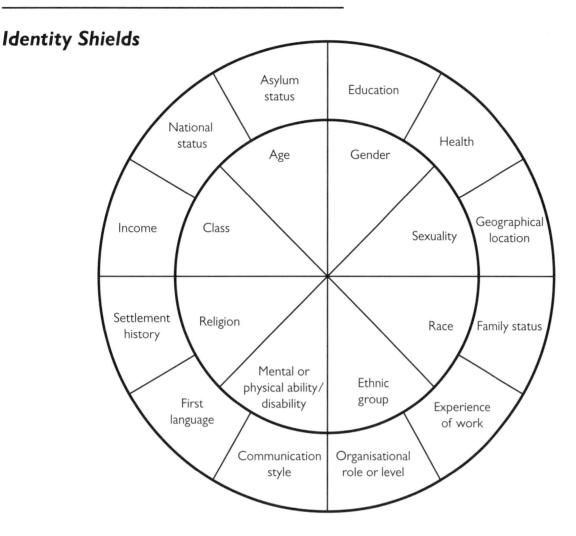

The Diversity Wheel shows both primary (inner circle) and secondary (outer circle) dimensions of diversity which have an impact on each of us at home, at work and in society. It is the interaction between these dimensions that influences self-image, values, opportunities and expectations.

Primary or core dimensions

People are usually most sensitive about these; most primary dimensions are visible, so projections can be made on this basis and people may immediately be subject to the stereotyped view of others.

Secondary dimensions

These are generally less visible and may contain a greater element of choice. They may change throughout our lives and so, because we acquire, discard and modify many of these dimensions, their influence on our lives is less constant and more individualised than is true for the primary dimensions.

The Diversity Wheel is adapted from Loden (1996) and was originally devised by Marilyn Loden and Julie Rosener.

Exercise 5.5 Dominant and Subordinate Groups

Time: 50 min.

Description

A small group exercise to explore how differences in power in society manifest.

Aims

To consider which groups are dominant in our society. To explore how particular groups maintain dominance. To compare participants' personal experience within society.

Directions

1. In advance prepare one set of sticky notes (see the Handout for Exercise 5.5) and one sheet of flipchart paper for each group of four to five people. The flipchart sheet should be divided lengthways into one narrow column headed 'Dominant Group' and one wider column headed 'Subordinate Groups'. Set up stations around the room so that each group can work privately.

2. Ask the group what comes to mind when they hear the word 'dominant'. Ask them what comes to mind when they hear the word 'subordinate'. Explain that they will be given sticky notes listing many of the different groups in UK society covering areas such as gender, class and status. From each cluster of identities, they need to decide which group is dominant in our society, placing that sticky note in the Dominant column, and arrange the rest of the notes for that category in order of decreasing dominance in the Subordinate column.   **23 min.**

3. After they have allocated the sticky notes, ask them to identify what criteria they used to decide which group fitted where and list these on a piece of flipchart paper.   **5 min.**

4. There will be 16 groups listed under 'Dominant Groups'. Explain that participants get one point for each of these groups they belong to. Ask them to write down their total and then to share that total with the other members of their group.   **2 min.**

5. In their groups, ask the participants to discuss whether they felt that their scores reflected their personal experience of how powerful or otherwise they feel in their lives and to think about whether there are some groupings that are so powerful in our society that they should have a higher score than one point.   **5 min.**

Feedback and discussion

Did participants feel more or less powerful than their scores? Why? Which groups control our society? How do these dominant groups hold power over subordinate groups? How do subordinate groups react to this domination?   **15 min.**

Notes

Dominant groups maintain control over subordinate groups by defining what is normal, making the rules, labelling others, exaggerating differences and restricting entry to their group. Members of subordinate groups may react to this by disconnecting or separating themselves from the dominant group or by becoming more like the dominant group.

This exercise focuses on 'positional power' in society, that is, the power people have by virtue of being a member of a particular group. An individual's sense of power may vary depending on their sense of their personal power. This exercise can bring up strong negative feelings; for example, white, middle-class men hold high group positional power in society, yet a white, middle-class man might not feel this personally and may want to reject any association with the power that comes with being a member of the group. Alternatively, a young Asian woman would not hold high group positional power in society and may resist the idea that we live in a patriarchal society. If emotions have been stirred, give participants an opportunity to talk through their response to the exercise in pairs. You can link this to Exercise 3.3, Positional versus Personal Power.

Skills

Listening. Cooperation. Self-awareness and group awareness. Analysis.

Handout – Briefing Sheet for Exercise 5.5

Dominant and Subordinate Groups

Listed below are 16 areas of difference between us. Write the name of each small group on one sticky note; there should therefore be one for male, one for female, one for black, etc. You will need 51 sticky notes per group. Try to use large sticky notes and write with a flipchart pen.

- Male/female
- Black/white/Asian/dual heritage
- Gay/lesbian/bisexual/transgender/heterosexual
- Youth/adult/elderly
- Christian/Muslim/Jewish/Sikh/Hindu/Buddhist/Atheist
- Not employed/employed
- Single/civil partner/married/co-habitant
- Child-free/parent
- People with disability/People without disability
- Northerner/Southerner
- Working class/middle class/upper class
- Grew up in care system/grew up in family
- Scottish/English/Welsh/Northern Irish
- Asylum seeker/refugee/temporary resident/UK national
- English is first language/English is not first language
- University educated/completed secondary school/didn't complete school

(Amend as appropriate for the group.)

Exercise 5.6 Breaking the Code

Time: 25 min.

Description

A group exercise exploring the impact of being outside the group.

Aims

To experience being outside the group. To experience being part of the in-group. To identify group norms or codes.

Directions

1. Ask a volunteer to leave the room. The remainder of the participants think of something physical they will do when having a discussion (or performing some other agreed activity) in front of the person who is outside the room. **3 min.**

2. The volunteer comes back into the room and starts a careful observation of the group, who are following the agreed strategy. When the outsider feels they have 'broken the code' they start to use the code themselves and interact with the group. If they are correct the group will accept them as one of their own; if they are mistaken the group will continue to ignore them. Allow them three attempts to break the code. **4 min.**

3. Another group member should now have a turn. The group can make the code more difficult and sophisticated every time they repeat the exercise. **10 min.**

Feedback and discussion

How did the outsider feel? What is it like trying to gain entry to a closed group? What did they discover when trying to crack the code? How did the group members feel during the exercise? What messages do closed groups give outsiders? Why do people need closed groups? How does this exercise relate to what happens in everyday life? **8 min.**

Notes

It is common when running this exercise for participants to take particular pleasure in excluding the person outside the room. Being part of a majority can lead to people feeling safe, comfortable and powerful in relation to others. They may also want to protect that group or keep other people out in order to preserve the identity of the group and those feelings of safety, comfort and power. In turn, being isolated can lead to feelings of insecurity, danger and loneliness. People can be excluded in many ways other than physically.

Skills

Careful observation. Teamwork and group planning. Concentration. Courage.

Exercise 5.7 Privilege

Time: 40 min.

Description

A paired sharing exercise in which participants reflect on how different aspects of their identity might have privileged them.

Aims

To explore the notion of privilege in relation to identity. For participants to reflect on aspects of their own identity that might have afforded them privileges in their lives.

Directions

1. Ask participants to wordstorm the word privilege. What do they think when they hear it? When they think about different identities which do they think are privileged and which not?   **5 min.**

2. Ask participants to divide into pairs and to share the key aspects of their identity that they discussed in Exercise 5.4, Identity Shields.   **5 min.**

3. Individually, each participant should write two lists: the first records all the ways that their own identity has afforded them certain privileges; the second lists all the ways their partner's identity may have afforded them certain privileges.   **10 min.**

4. Partners choose who is going first. The first participant shares their list of the ways they have been privileged by their identity. Their partner listens and then together they discuss any additions from the list their partner made about them.   **5 min.**

5. Ask partners to swap roles and repeat Stage 4.   **5 min.**

Feedback and discussion

What is it like to think about the notion of privilege in relation to identity? Were there any privileges that your partners spotted about your identity that you weren't aware of? How comfortable are you with thinking of yourself as privileged by your identity? Are some people more privileged than others? How might privilege influence what you can or cannot do? What feelings do you notice have been aroused when discussing this subject?   **10 min.**

Notes

It may be important to distinguish between perceived personal or social privileges – for example, women are more likely to be allowed through a door first – and privilege on an institutional or societal level – for example, men are still more likely to be paid more than women and are more likely to be given a pay rise if they ask for one.

It is also interesting to explore how comfortable we are acknowledging the privilege that our identity can give us; for example, a white woman may be less likely to be stopped by the police on the street in the UK than a black man.

Skills

Listening. Self-awareness. Empathy.

Exercise 5.8 Culture Pyramid

Time: 35 min.

Description

A whole-group exercise exploring visible and invisible aspects of culture.

Aims

To explore how we see our own culture. To consider whether we may see our own culture as much more complex than those of other people.

Directions

1. If you have time before the session, ask the participants to bring with them one item of cultural significance that they can share with the group. Start the exercise by sharing these items and why they are important. Then ask the participants to wordstorm as many aspects of culture as they can think of, writing each one on a sticky note. Place the sticky notes on a sheet of flipchart paper on the wall beside the flipchart. **20 min.**

2. Draw a large extended pyramid shape on a piece of flipchart paper, with the apex at the top of the page. Draw a line across the middle of the pyramid. Above the line represents those aspects of culture that are visible; below the line represents those aspects of culture that are invisible.

3. Ask the participants to decide where to place each of the sticky notes: above or below the line. **5 min.**

Feedback and discussion

What aspects of your culture are more important to you – the visible or the invisible? Why is that? Do we make assumptions about the values of other members of our own group? When we meet people from other cultures, at which level (visible or invisible) do we tend to engage with them? Do we simplify the cultural values of other groups? **10 min.**
Further questions:

*   Can you think about a time when you were in a group of people and felt that you really belonged? Why was that?

*   Have you had the opposite experience?

Notes

Further questions might focus on the sense of belonging we may or may not experience as part of a cultural group. Culture can be expressed visibly through music, language, food, dress, art, etc. However, culture is also about the shared rituals, symbols and practices that give a group a sense of identity. Each group tends to see their cultural ways as the 'norm' and to interpret the actions of others according to their group's values or 'codes of behaviour'. This can lead to misunderstanding and conflict. Culture both influences the way people behave and is influenced by people's behaviour and so is continually evolving. The organisation Responding to Conflict believes that 'Culture does much to determine the way people think and act. They honour their own culture, and often seek to maintain it in the face of outside influences.'

Skills

Sharing personal information. Listening. Empathy.

Exercise 5.9 History of the Word

Time: 25 min.

Description

A small-group exercise exploring the evolution of the language that has been used to label different groups.

Aims

To understand that the language used to label different groups is evolving. To broaden knowledge of language used about particular groups. To identify what are appropriate labels for groups.

Directions

1.   Prepare in advance sets of words that have been used to label particular groups. Possible groups might be: black people, people with disabilities, gay men, women, people of dual heritage. Try to find as many words as you can for each group and write the words on sheets of A4 paper. Prepare one set for each small group.

2.   Ask participants to get into groups of four or five. Give each group a set of labels and ask them to arrange the labels in order of when that label was first used to describe the group through to the most current label. If they are not familiar with any of the words, they can ask other members of the group or yourself.   **15 min.**

Feedback and discussion

Where do these labels come from? What is the intention of these labels? Are there links between this exercise and Exercise 5.5, Dominant and Subordinate Groups? Why is it important to know about language?   **10 min.**

Notes

The timeline is more illustrative of the evolution of language rather than historically accurate. Although language is continually evolving, there are generally accepted labels for each group. It is important to highlight these rather than focusing on personal levels of acceptance/tolerance. Context is also important; for example, in the UK we would generally not use the word 'coloured' to describe a black person, whereas in the USA black people may be identified as 'people of color', and in South Africa the term 'coloured' is used for people of dual heritage. An extension of this exercise would be 'hotspots'. Take a sample of the words used and place them one at a time in the middle of the room. Ask the participants to place themselves in relation to the word – if they find the word utterly offensive they should place themselves near the word; if they do not feel so strongly about the word they should place themselves further away. Ask people to speak about why they have placed themselves where they have.

Skills

Listening. Verbal articulacy. Drawing out information. Cooperation.

Exercise 5.10 Reclaiming or Sustaining

Time: 25 min.

Description

A small-group exercise to explore the advantages and disadvantages of using derogatory terms within groups.

Aims

To consider the advantages and disadvantages of subordinate groups reclaiming labels that historically have been used in a derogatory way.

Directions

1.   Highlight the practice in some groups of calling each other terms that have traditionally been used in a derogatory way to label that group, when group members would not accept an outsider calling them by that term. Examples might be young women calling themselves 'slapper' or 'bitch', young Pakistani men calling themselves 'Paki' and young black men calling each other 'nigger'. Ask the group to suggest why groups might do this.
5 min.

2.   Draw an imaginary line across the room. Mark one end 'Reclaiming' and the other 'Sustaining'. Ask the participants to position themselves somewhere along the line that most reflects how they view this behaviour. Ask people to give their reasons for placing themselves where they did.
10 min.

Feedback and discussion

Give the participants a copy of Handout for Exercise 5.10, Reclaiming or Sustaining. Should they challenge this habit or not when it occurs?
10 min.

Notes

It is likely that there will be a range of opinions about whether or not to challenge this behaviour; some people will argue that the group is reclaiming the word for themselves whilst others will feel strongly that by using the word they are keeping it in circulation. It may be useful to link this back to Exercise 5.5, Dominant and Subordinate Groups as these tend to be labels created by dominant groups to suppress subordinate groups. For participants who are working in teams at work, it is important to have a consistent strategy of challenging or not challenging to give a clear message to young people.

Skills

Self-awareness and group awareness. Listening skills. Analysis.

Handout for Exercise 5.10

Reclaiming or Sustaining

Arguments for and against groups using derogatory labels within their own groups

For:

- By using it themselves they are taking the impact or sting out of the comment; they are inoculating themselves.
- They know they are using the word to denote commonality.
- They use the words to form their own 'in-group' which then excludes others.
- They believe they are reclaiming the word for themselves.
- They believe they can 'wash' the word clean.
- It is important to separate the word and the intention.
- They are free to choose their own labels.
- It is part of the process of releasing internalised oppression.

Against:

- Many of these words were developed by dominant groups to marginalise other groups; they are not words that the group would have used to label themselves, so they are not theirs to reclaim.
- Users may not be aware of the history of the word.
- There is a double standard: one rule for us, one rule for others, which perpetuates in-groups and out-groups.
- There is the possibility of misunderstanding the word.
- Using the label keeps the word in circulation.
- It is not possible to separate the word from its history.
- Other members of the group may have fought hard against prejudice and discrimination to have these labels taken out of circulation.
- There is the drip-drip effect on self-esteem of using negative labels to describe yourself.

Exercise 5.11 Defining Inappropriate Language

Time: 30 min.

Description

An exercise identifying specific examples of inappropriate language and behaviour in a work context and developing a rationale for challenging these remarks.

Aims

To develop a common understanding of what is inappropriate language and behaviour. To understand why it is important to challenge inappropriate language or remarks. To consider what might prevent us from challenging what others say.

Directions

1. Wordstorm as many examples as possible of inappropriate language and behaviour that participants may come across in their work. Ask the group to focus on disrespectful words or phrases about other groups of people. Keep going until the whole of one sheet of flipchart paper is covered. If participants are reticent in coming up with ideas, give them some examples from your own work. **10 min.**

2. Ask participants to work in pairs to discuss which of the remarks they would challenge and why; which remarks they are more or less likely to hear and why; and what might stop them from challenging remarks. **10 min.**

Feedback and discussion

Which remarks are participants more likely to challenge and why? Which remarks are they less likely to challenge and why? What stops them from challenging some remarks? What criteria should they use for deciding when to intervene? **10 min.**

Notes

When one aspect of our identity is particularly important to us, we are more likely to be alert to disrespectful language about that group; conversely, if we are not a member of a particular group, we may be less aware of disrespectful remarks made about that group. A useful guide for deciding whether or not to challenge is to consider what the intention of the remark (whether conscious or unconscious) might have been and what the effect of the comment might be on someone from that group whether they are present at the time or not. You can link this exercise back to the exercise on Dominant and Subordinate groups; inappropriate remarks are often made by dominant groups to maintain their supremacy. Refer participants to Handout for Exercise 5.11, Allport's Scale of Prejudice and the following quote:

First they came for the communists, and I did not speak out—

because I was not a communist;

Then they came for the socialists, and I did not speak out—

because I was not a socialist;

Then they came for the trade unionists, and I did not speak out—

because I was not a trade unionist;

Then they came for the Jews, and I did not speak out—

because I was not a Jew;

Then they came for me—

and there was no one left to speak out for me.

Martin Niemöller

Martin Niemöller was a German, anti-Nazi theologian and Lutheran pastor. Because of his opposition to the Nazi state control of the churches, he was imprisoned in the concentration camps from 1937 until 1945. After his release he expressed his deep regret for not having done more to help the victims of the Nazis. He is best known as the author of this poem.

Skills

Concentration. Group acceptance of ideas. Self-reflection.

Handout for Exercise 5.11

Defining Inappropriate Language

Allport's Scale of Prejudice

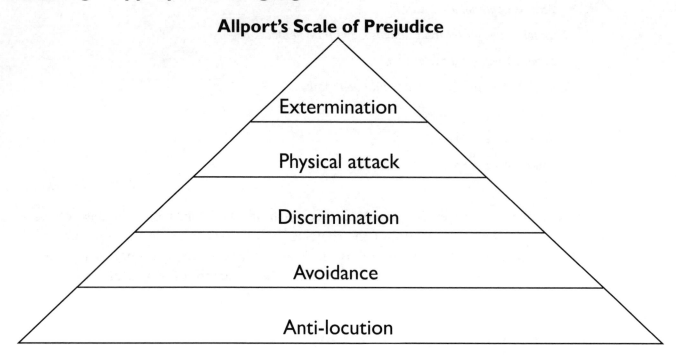

Allport's Scale of Prejudice (1954) was drawn up in response to the Holocaust. Whilst this is an extreme example of human behaviour, the model can be used to understand how prejudice can develop from relatively low-level actions into much more serious divisive activities if it is not challenged early. In this model each level feeds the stage above it. The model can be applied to the treatment of an individual or a particular group of people at social, institutional and societal levels. Inversely individuals, institutions, communities and the State need to be involved in challenging prejudice. The five levels of Allport's Scale of Prejudice are defined as follows:

- **Anti-locution** (bad-mouthing): prejudice is expressed through name-calling, put-downs, stereotyping, rumours, or inappropriate humour or jokes.

- **Avoidance**: individuals or groups are marginalised or ostracised, either deliberately or unintentionally. This could include avoiding or excluding people and reflects the development of insiders and outsiders.

- **Discrimination** (prejudice in action): rules (written or unwritten) or laws may start to legitimise the unfair treatment of others in areas such as education, housing and employment.

- **Physical attack**: this could include threats, assaults, arson, vandalism, desecration, murder and what is currently known as hate crime.

- **Extermination**: this is the deliberate, systematic extermination of a group of people, currently recognised as ethnic cleansing.

Exercise 5.12 Challenge Carousel: Talk to the Hand 'Cos the Face Ain't Listening

Time: 45 min.

Description

A paired exercise rehearsing a range of responses to inappropriate or derogatory language.

Aims

To develop a range of creative responses to derogatory language. To practise responding to inappropriate language in the moment.

Directions

1. Use the list of inappropriate expressions or phrases from Exercise 5.11, Defining Inappropriate Language. Ask the group to come up with a range of responses to challenge these remarks and record them on the flipchart. Ask them what their intention would be in challenging these remarks. **10 min.**

2. If necessary trainers can demonstrate both ineffective and effective ways of challenging the remarks. **3 min.**

3. Arrange the seating so that there are two concentric circles of chairs, with the inner circle facing outwards and the outer circle facing inwards. The chairs should be facing each other, so there should be an equal number of chairs on the inner and outer circles. Participants should each sit on a chair. **2 min.**

4. The participants in the inner circle will take on the role of a young person; their task will be to make an inappropriate remark, using one of the phrases from the flipchart. The role of the outer circle is to challenge the remarks, with a view to opening up a dialogue with the young person rather than closing them down. They can use the ideas generated earlier in the exercise. Give the pair two minutes for the dialogue before calling them to a halt and asking the members of the inner circle to move one place to the right so they have a new responder. Ask them to choose a new phrase to challenge their new responder. **10 min.**

5. When the members of the inner circle have challenged all the members of the outer circle, the participants should swap roles. The members of the outer circle will therefore take on the role of a young person and make the inappropriate remarks, and the members of the inner circle will have an opportunity to challenge these remarks. **10 min.**

Feedback and discussion

Ask participants to identify what interventions worked and why. Then ask them to identify which interventions were not so successful and why. You can add new ideas to the list on the flipchart. Ask them to draw on their experience of playing a young person and what they can learn from taking on that role. **10 min.**

Notes

You may want to remind participants about the work they did in Exercise 2.6, Red Labels. The aim of the exercise is to explore ways to open up a dialogue with a young person so they can think about the remarks they are making. There are many different strategies for doing this; a useful framework for thinking about challenging might be:

Affirmation	Illumination
'Thanks for raising the issue; I wonder what it is like to be a refugee in this country.'	'That's not my experience of women drivers. I find it difficult when I am stereotyped as I would like to be seen as an individual. When have you been seen as being the same as others in your group?'
Exploration	**Information**
'What was your intention in making that remark? Who decides if something is a joke? What might be the impact on someone who was gay?'	'When you say they are taking all our jobs, who do you mean by "they"? Where did you get that information from? Is everything you read on the internet true?'

It may be useful to remind participants that when they are role-playing a young person, they should respond to what their partner says and not get 'locked into' being unresponsive.

Skills

Creativity. Active listening. Drawing out information. Empathy. Acting and thinking under pressure.

Chapter 6

The Blaze

Crisis Management, Recovery and Reparation

There is no shortage of logs to bring up the blaze. The flames leap and the fire rages. The logs are consumed by the flames. The huge blaze burns and it consumes all it touches. But it can also be a force for regeneration, a catalyst for new growth. The conflict blazes. There is damage and pain. Some are burnt by the fire; some are standing well clear of it. But no one is untouched by the blazing conflict.

Once a fire is in full blaze the options are limited: we run away from it, try to put it out or run into it. The third option looks suicidal, but there are those who walk into flames confident that they will be unharmed. We can take on the role of firefighter, dress ourselves in flame-resistant clothing, enter the fire and remain unscathed. Firefighters can enter blazing conflicts, and although they may be affected by what happens they should not be harmed. This third option is not about putting the fire out; it is about showing the way out of it to those who are in the middle. When we are in the middle of a blaze, the smoke and fumes overcome us, and the exit route may not be clear. Firefighters, mediators, peacebuilders, facilitators and defusers can all lead the way to the escape route for those who want to take it. What will make us flame-proof? What are the exits that we offer others? What role can we play to calm or defuse the heat? How can we help turn the blaze of a destructive conflict into the creative energy of change and progress?

Focus

Conflict escalation; conflict analysis; coping in a crisis; recovery from a crisis; creating safety.

Key concepts

Conflict analysis; clarifying roles; dealing with mistakes; crisis and change; recovery and reparation.

Key questions

What goes on in a crisis situation? What lies at the roots of destructive behaviour? What do we need to survive and recover from crisis, personally and professionally? What strategies can we create to ensure the workplace is safe? How can I work together with others to prevent further damage and repair the harm?

The Blaze

Exercise 6.1 Throwing the Stone

Time: 55 min.

Description

A small-group role-play exercise exploring the possible reasons behind a violent incident.

Aims

To uncover the causal sequence behind a seemingly random act of violence. To explore the motives behind the act. To look for alternatives to violent behaviour.

Directions

1.   Divide participants into groups of about six or seven. Each group will create and act out a story. The stories end with the same picture: a person holding a stone and about to throw it at a window.

2.   All the groups create their story by answering these questions about that picture:

     ◦   Is there any significance in the stone thrower's choice of this particular window?

     ◦   Is the person alone? If not, who are they with?

     ◦   If others are present, are they involved in any way?

     ◦   What was the final straw that led to the decision to break the window?

     ◦   Where did that take place?

     ◦   What led up to that? Who else was involved?

     ◦   What incidents helped to create the feelings and frustrations behind the incident?

     The group needs to draw out the basics of their story, divide up the roles and prepare the scenes, ending with a frozen picture of a stone about to be thrown.   **10 min.**

3.   The groups act out their scenes for each other. Ask for feedback from the audience about what they perceive is actually going on. What is at the root? The role-play might end, for example, with a child throwing a stone through a school staffroom window, and we might have been shown scenes that tell us that she was falsely accused of stealing and suspended from school for a week. So at the root of the incident could lie thoughts of not being listened to and not being believed and intense feelings of injustice, isolation, inadequacy and anger.   **10 min.**

4.   In the same groups, ask participants to think about ways of addressing the roots of the incident, focusing on whether there is a pattern of behaviour and, if there is, how it could be changed. Below are some useful questions to consider. You could use these in discussion with a group once they have come up with their own ideas.

     Finding a pattern of behaviour: Has a similar incident happened before? Is it likely to happen again?

     Changing a pattern of behaviour: What outside forces could prevent it from happening again? What could the stone thrower do to stop responding in the same way? What are possible alternative responses? What would be helpful responses from friends and onlookers?   **15 min.**

5.   Participants should come together to share these ideas and develop them into a checklist.   **10 min.**

Feedback and discussion

Participants might consider the following questions. Do you understand why the stone is being thrown? Do you have any sympathy with the perpetrator? What is the difference between understanding and sympathising? What factors escalated the situation for the young person? What or who could have de-escalated the situation? What roles did other people take in the situation?   **10 min.**

Notes

Whilst this exercise focuses on the perpetrator, it could also be used to explore the role of the bystanders. This exercise can be useful with a young person who is aware of destructive cycles and wants to change them. If there has been a violent incident, in a youth club, for instance, this exercise could be used to find out what people thought about it. Use the structure, but end the scene by freezing on the incident you want to focus on. Adapt the questions to make them relevant. When this exercise is done with young people, the questions will raise real issues for them and bring out deeply felt responses. You can use the exercise to find out what young people are experiencing in relation to these questions, without directly questioning them about their personal lives.

Skills

Imaginative story-building. Group listening and idea-building. Accepting other people's ideas and enacting them.

Exercise 6.2 Conflict Timeline

Time: 45 min.

Description

A group exercise to examine the history of a particular conflict and how it has developed over time.

Aims

To develop awareness of the historical context for conflict. To understand how a conflict develops over time and can be impacted on by geographical, economic, demographic and local-policy change.

Directions

1.   Divide participants into small groups. Ask each group to come up with an example of a conflict in the community or local area involving young people that they have some knowledge of and would like to explore further.   **5 min.**

2.   In their small groups ask participants to divide up according to the number of parties involved. So, for example, with a conflict involving two rival groups of young people who are having a dispute about territory, they would divide into two smaller groups. Ask each group to draw a timeline of the history of the conflict from the perspective of that group of young people. Make sure that both groups identify the wider factors that have impacted on the conflict, as well as the points where the conflict escalated because of an action by an individual or a group. These could be, for example, the closure of a youth centre which was on neutral ground and allowed the two groups to come together peaceably; a new housing development in the area which has meant that one of the groups has been pushed out of an area they felt belonged to them; a change in policing strategy, etc. A timeline could span 50 years, 5 months or 5 days; the group can choose the time span they want to cover according to the nature of the conflict and the relevance of the different impacting factors they identify.   **15 min.**

3.   Ask the groups to analyse the different timelines they have created. What are the differences and similarities? What have been the wider neighbourhood and area factors that have most influenced the development of the conflict? What change in the local area or neighbourhood could most positively impact on the conflict?   **15 min.**

Feedback and discussion

What are the wider factors influencing conflict in local communities? How can we use this information to help calm, defuse or prevent community conflict? How can understanding the wider context of a conflict situation support us in our work with young people?   **10 min.**

Notes

Plotting events along a timeline can help us understand the dynamics of what has happened over time and how that impacts on a current conflict involving young people in the local community. Conflict in communities can be impacted by changes in the geography (for example, a new road being built which divides a community in two); in the demographics (the influx of a new group or community into a settled area); in local economics (for example, increased unemployment because of the closure of a local call centre); and in local policy (a crackdown on anti-social behaviour in the area). Although on their own none of these factors would necessarily lead to conflict, they can impact conflict indirectly.

This exercise was originally developed by the organisation Responding to Conflict (Fisher *et al.* 1998).

Skills

Analysis. Teamwork. Planning. Accepting other people's ideas.

Exercise 6.3 Mapping a Conflict

Time: 55 min.

Description

A small-group exercise exploring conflict using a visual tool for mapping relationships between affected parties.

Aims

To identify all the different parties directly or indirectly involved in conflict. To analyse the relationships between different parties. To devise strategies for working constructively with a conflict situation.

Directions

1. Divide participants into small groups. Ask each group to choose an example of a conflict involving young people that they have some knowledge of and would like to explore further. Participants can use the examples that they identified in Exercise 6.2, Conflict Timeline. **5 min.**

2. Each group should identify all the different groups involved in the conflict, whether or not they are involved in the conflict directly or have a role to play in the local area. **5 min.**

3. Give each group a copy of Handout 1 for Exercise 6.3, Mapping a Conflict and explain the different symbols. Each group will then map out their conflict using the symbols suggested. (See the example in Handout 2 for Exercise 6.3, Example Map.) **15 min.**

4. When they have finished, ask each group to discuss the following questions: How did they decide on the size of circle for each group? What relationships could be strengthened or developed? Are any key relationships missing? What can be done to address the conflict? Who can best do it? What groundwork needs to be laid beforehand? What structures need to be built afterwards? What kinds of short-, medium- and long-term strategies need to be put into place? **20 min.**

Feedback and discussion

What did participants learn from mapping the conflict visually? What kind of strategies did participants develop to address the conflict? How might participants use this in their work? **10 min.**

Notes

This tool provides a snapshot of a conflict at a fixed point in time. It can be used again at a later date to check whether an intervention has made a difference. Focusing attention on the relationships surrounding the actual conflict encourages a more strategic approach to conflict situations. For instance, with the example given on the handout there is no relationship between the youth service and the police, gang 1 or the school. Strengthening these relationships might mean that the staff at the youth service could foster better relationships with both gangs involved in the conflict.

It can also be used as a third-party intervention tool with all parties involved in the conflict creating their own map of the situation as they see it and then, with their permission, their map being shared with the other parties. This can lead to some surprising insights and revelations about how parties view themselves and each other. This could be the beginning of fostering a greater understanding between parties.

This exercise was originally developed by the organisation Responding to Conflict (Fisher *et al*. 1998) and has been used in their international work to help analyse conflict situations. It can be used to map any kind of conflict – from one involving individuals, to family conflict, to violent conflict affecting nations.

Skills

Analysis. Teamwork.

Handout I for Exercise 6.3

Mapping a Conflict

Key

The size of the circle represents the power of that party.

A single line represents a relationship.

A double line represents an alliance.

A line with an arrow represents the direction of influence.

A dotted line represents a weak relationship or intermittent link.

A jagged line represents a conflict.

A bar across a straight line indicates a previous relationship which no longer exists or is now problematic.

Handout 2 for Exercise 6.3

Mapping a Conflict

Example map

Example of a conflict between two rival gangs of young people:

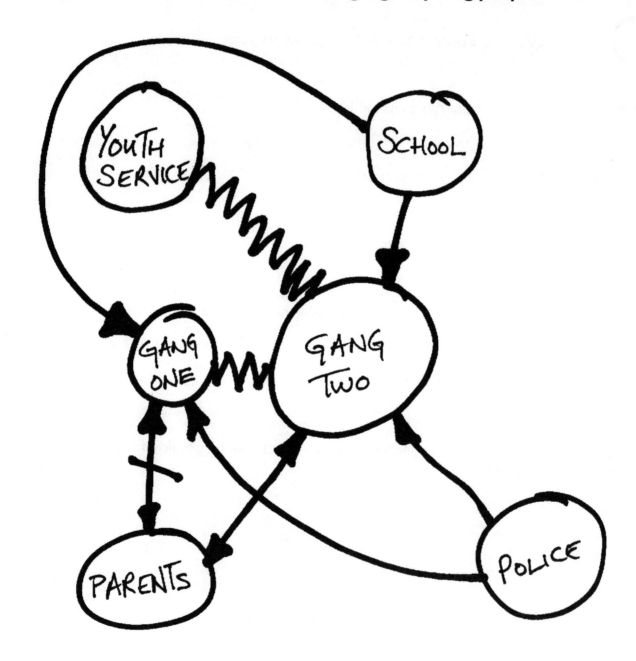

Exercise 6.4 The ABC Triangle

Time: 55 min.

Description

A small-group exercise exploring the major components of youth conflict situations.

Aims

To identify three major components of youth conflict situations. To clarify the impact these can have on a situation of conflict. To develop awareness of how the relationship between different parties' attitudes, behaviour and contexts can influence the development of conflict.

Directions

1. Give everyone a copy of the Handout for Exercise 6.4, The ABC Triangle and talk it through, answering any questions. Divide the participants into groups of four or five. Within each group, one participant volunteers a conflict situation that they have some knowledge of. This does not have to be a conflict that they are directly involved in but simply one in which they know some of the arguments of the different parties. This could be, for example, a conflict between a group of young people and a group of residents on a local estate. **10 min.**

2. In small groups identify the different parties involved in the conflict. Make a separate ABC triangle for each of the different parties listing their attitudes, behaviours and context from their viewpoint. **10 min.**

3. In the centre of each triangle identify what the most important *needs* and/or *fears* are for that party. **5 min.**

4. Compare the differences and similarities for each party, and notice how each party's attitudes, behaviours and context are impacting on the other parties. **10 min.**

5. Discuss and devise a strategy for helping the parties to address the conflict between them. **15 min.**

Feedback and discussion

What do you notice about the differences and similarities between the different parties? What practical strategies did participants formulate? How might participants use this tool in their work? **5 min.**

Notes

This exercise was originally developed by the organisation Responding to Conflict (Fisher *et al.* 1998). It can be used to analyse conflict situations between individuals but is particularly useful for analysing conflict between different groups at a community level. Parties can use it to analyse their own group's role in a conflict situation and also to understand how the other parties are impacting on their own behaviour. It can be used as a third-party intervention tool, for example, by working with the different parties separately and then asking their permission to share their triangles with the other parties so that each party gains more understanding of the conflict. Used with other conflict analysis tools – particularly Exercises 6.2, Conflict Timeline, and 6.3, Mapping a Conflict, it can help develop a strategy for addressing a protracted or difficult conflict.

Skills

Analysis. Teamwork.

Handout for Exercise 6.4

The ABC Triangle

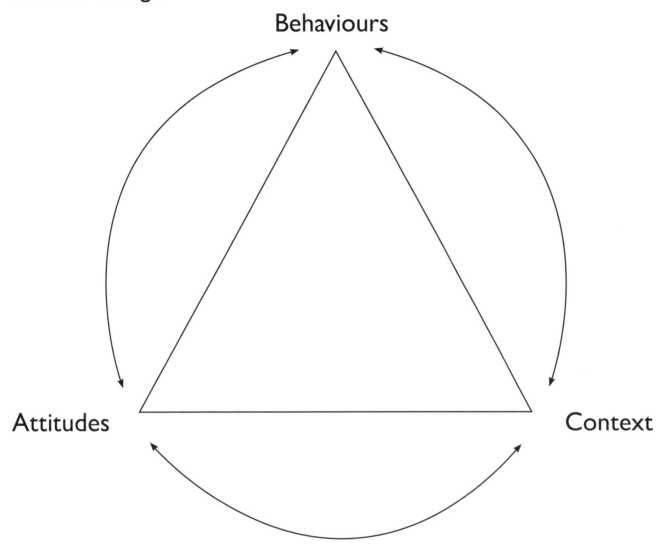

This analysis is based on the premise that conflicts have three major components: the context or the situation, the behaviour of those involved and their attitudes. These are represented graphically as the corners of a triangle.

These three factors influence each other – hence the arrows leading from one to another. The behaviour of one group can influence the attitude of another. If we take the example given in the exercise of a conflict between a group of young people and residents on a local estate, if the residents on the estate are unfriendly and unwelcoming towards the young people, then the young people may react by becoming hostile towards the residents. This attitude can then have an effect on the context; the young people become so hostile that the residents demand that CCTV cameras are installed on the estate. This change in the physical environment will in turn affect each group's behaviour and attitudes and so on. If the situation is to improve then one or, more likely, all of these will have to change.

Exercise 6.5 Positions, Interests, Needs

Time: 30 min.

Description

An interactive group exercise analysing the interests and needs of different parties in conflict.

Aims

To identify the underlying drivers for conflict. To explore what disputing parties have in common in order to build agreement.

Directions

1. Divide participants into small groups. Ask each group to identify a conflict situation to explore further. Using Handout for Exercise 6.5, Positions, Interests, Needs, talk through how positions, interests and needs might be identified. Ask participants to draw out the triangles on a large piece of paper. **10 min.**

2. Each group identifies the positions, interests and needs of the two parties in conflict, identifying areas of shared interests and needs that could begin to form the basis of a negotiation. **15 min.**

Feedback and discussion

What did you discover about areas of shared interests and needs? What might be the basis for an agreement between the two parties? How else might you use this tool? **5 min.**

Notes

If you have time you can put this exercise on its feet to get an idea of how the conversation can shift once you begin to explore what lies beneath the different parties' positions. Ask two groups to represent two parties in conflict. One person from each group stands up and expresses the position of their party. Follow this up with one person from each group standing up and expressing the interests of their party and end with one person from each group standing up and expressing the needs of their party. You could experiment with a third party intervening and attempting to negotiate on the basis of the interests and needs.

Handout for Exercise 6.5

Positions, Interests, Needs

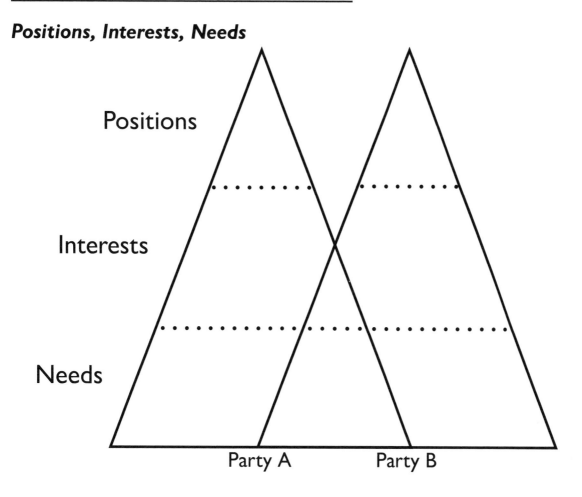

In the section marked Positions write down what the different parties are **saying they want**. In the section marked Interests write down what the different parties **really want**. In the section marked Needs write down what the different parties **actually need**. Needs tend to be the non-negotiable basic human needs, such as safety, security, the right to be treated with respect and dignity, etc.

When you begin to unpick the interests and needs that underlie what the different parties are saying you should begin to move closer to identifying shared interests and needs – in the area where the triangles overlap.

As the parties begin to negotiate on the basis of interests, rather than positions, they develop more trust and a greater understanding of the needs of the other party as well as of their own. This may lead them to identify more and more areas of need which they have in common.

This model was originally developed by Andrew Acland (1990).

Exercise 6.6 What's My Role?

Time: 30 min.

Description

A whole-group exercise to explore the range of roles youth work professionals can use to empower young people.

Aims

To identify both formal and informal roles within the remit of a youth work professional. To explore the distinctions between these roles.

Directions

1. Ask participants to write down four words or short phrases on separate sticky notes to describe how they see themselves as youth work professionals in relation to the young people they work with: how would they describe what they do; what roles do they take on; how would they characterise their way of working? **5 min.**

2. The participants now share their lists with a partner. What would they say was their key modus operandi? What does this mean they do or do not do in their work? Does this change when they are in stressful or conflict situations? **5 min.**

3. Possible roles identified might include: friend, teacher, trainer, referee, shoulder to cry on, coach, mediator, boss, educator. Using a continuum with Friend (I am your mate; I am one of you; we are all in this together) at one end and Authority (I am the boss; I decide what happens here; you will do what I say) at the other, ask the participants to place their sticky notes on the line where they think it fits. This can be done on a piece of flipchart paper, on the wall or along the ground. **10 min.**

Feedback and discussion

What are the advantages and disadvantages of the Friend and Authority roles for the participants and for the young people they work with? How important is it to be consistent in their approach to young people? **10 min.**

Notes

Many people working with young people will oscillate between the informal roles of friend and authority. You can be swayed by a need to be liked, to feel important, to gain control or to have a young person do what you say. This can be confusing for young people. It is important to offer a clear, consistent and boundaried approach in order to promote safety and model responsibility. In order to do that you need to consider regularly the purpose of your role and the intention of any conversation you have within it.

Skills

Honesty. Exploration. Self-reflection.

Exercise 6.7 Personal and Professional

Time: 40 min.

Description

A small-group exercise exploring our personal and professional personas at work.

Aims

To explore how much of ourselves we bring to our professional work. To consider the distinctions between our personal and professional personas. To articulate the boundaries between our personas.

Directions

1. Write the following quotation on the flipchart:

    The key purpose of youth work is to: enable young people to develop holistically, working with them to facilitate their personal, social and educational development, to enable them to develop their voice, influence and place in society and to reach their full potential.

    This definition, as set down by the National Occupational Standards for Youth Work (Lifelong Learning UK 2007), breaks down into five first-level functions: facilitate the personal, social and educational development of young people; promote equality and young people's interests and welfare; work with others; develop youth work strategy and practice; lead and manage teams and individuals.

2. Divide participants into groups of three and ask them to consider the quotation and the five functions, and to discuss the following questions: How much of yourself do you need to bring to the role of youth worker in order to meet those goals? Can you separate yourself personally and professionally? What are the boundaries between the personal you and the professional you in your role as a youth worker? Where might the two come into conflict? What boundaries would you not cross?   **25 min.**

Feedback and discussion

Is it possible to separate yourself personally and professionally as a youth worker? What is it about the role of a youth worker that makes that more challenging?   **15 min.**

Notes

This exercise develops the work of the previous exercise in thinking about roles, and their importance in our relationships with young people. If we don't make some clear boundaries between our personal and professional lives then we risk confusing the young people that we work with, and our own burnout and fatigue. On the other hand, sometimes when we step over those boundaries we can create a relationship with a young person that can help them to make a real change or shift. Part of developing skills as a youth worker is understanding when we need to either hold the boundaries or be more fluid in order to support a young person.

Skills

Self-reflection. Listening. Considering.

Exercise 6.8 My Vision

Time: 70 min.

Description

Group tableau work to devise a strategy for improving a situation.

Aims

To clarify the results we want in a situation. To identify the actions we need to take in order to achieve the results we want.

Directions

1. Ask participants to think of a situation they would like to change or improve, or something they would like to achieve. For example, someone might like to develop a better relationship with a sibling, or achieve a personal sporting ambition such as running a marathon.
   5 min.

2. Divide participants into small groups. Ask them to sculpt a picture of the result they would like to achieve. Participants should work on making the image as detailed as possible.
   10 min.

3. Ask participants to share their tableau with the whole group.
   10 min.

4. Ask for a volunteer to do some more detailed work on their situation. Divide a large piece of paper into two columns headed 'Actions' and 'Result'. Using their tableau ask them to describe the image they have made, focusing on what it feels like to have achieved their goal and what else is possible for them now that they have done that. Write up their answers in the Result column.
   5 min.

5. Ask the participant what actions they need to take to create the desired result. Write these in the Actions column. Be sure to explore whether some of the actions will have to be done repeatedly, for example, run every day, use 'I' statements with their sibling, etc.
   5 min.

6. Back in their groups ask participants to help each other to identify the actions they need to take in order to achieve the results they would like.
   15 min.

7. Ask each participant to feed back the first action they will be taking and when they will do it.
   10 min.

Feedback and discussion

What did you gain from this? What is the benefit of separating actions from results? How could you use this elsewhere? What is the most difficult step for you to take in the whole process?
   10 min.

Notes

Visualising the results we want can help us when we are faced with our own resistance to change. For example if the result we want to achieve is to run a 10K race, visualising winning can help us get out of bed on a cold winter morning to go for a training run. In order for us to achieve results in any aspect of our lives, our actions need to be in line with the results we want to achieve. This is developed further in Exercise 6.9, From Present to Future.

Skills

Imagination. Physical expression. Teamwork. Planning.

Exercise 6.9 From Present to Future

Time: 60 min.

Description

Group tableau work to devise a strategy for improving participants' working environments.

Aims

To clarify aims and objectives within our working environments. To find ways of achieving them.

Directions

1. Divide participants into groups of four or five. Ask each group to create two pairs of tableaux on the theme of their working environment. One pair of tableaux will represent *What we see* and *What we'd like to see*; the other will represent *How we feel about it* and *How we'd like to feel about it*. Ask groups to look for elements of the workplace that they can all relate to. If they find it impossible to accommodate their different viewpoints within collective tableaux, they can create more than one tableau under each heading. **25 min.**

2. Ask the groups to share their tableaux with the whole group. Participants should describe their tableaux in detail. Divide a large sheet of paper into two columns headed 'Present', 'Actions' and 'Future'. Under the headings Present and Future write down the descriptions of what the tableaux look like and feel like, starting with the Present. **10 min.**

3. Recap and clarify what is desired for the future, and make sure that what is written under the Future heading is accurate. Pose the following questions one at a time: (1) How will we know when we've got there? Write the answers under the Future heading. (2) What are the Actions we need to take to achieve this? (3) What is the first thing I will do about it when I get to work tomorrow? Write the answers under the Actions heading. It may be appropriate to write individuals' names next to specific actions. **15 min.**

Feedback and discussion

What did the participants learn about their own and other people's visions of the future? What do they need to do individually and collectively to get there? What might get in the way? How will they maintain the shared vision? **10 min.**

Notes

This exercise develops the work begun in Exercise 6.8, My Vision. It is useful work to do with a staff team as it enables them to pin down where difficulties lie and to look at how the first step to changing a situation can be taken. It can also be adapted for use with young people to assess how they can go about achieving what they want. If a group has difficulty identifying the ways in which the present situation can be addressed, encourage participants to consider the specific incidents or conditions that caused it. The Action column will then show the responses to these specifics.

Skills

Imagination. Physical expression. Teamwork. Planning.

Exercise 6.10 Fire Drill

Time: 60 min.

Description

An exercise in small and large groups which works towards the creation of an emergency procedure for a staff group as well as for individuals to use in times of crisis.

Aims

To highlight the needs and fears of the staff in terms of personal safety. To determine the boundaries of responsibility and the expectations of management and staff. To work out a safety procedure for the benefit of staff as well as young people. To work out ways in which this procedure could be implemented and supported. To explore needs in relation to staff training.

Directions

1. Ask every member of the group to identify two fears they have in the work environment, especially in relation to situations that could get out of hand, and two needs they would have if their fears were to be realised. **5 min.**

2. Participants now read out their fears in turn, then their needs. Draw any common needs and fears together while they are being read out. For example: 'My fear is that I will lose control and make the situation worse' and 'My need is for other people to take over if I seem to be losing control' (facilitators could write these up for the group). At the end of the sharing session, with the help of the group, try to synthesise all the needs and fears into as few words as possible. **5 min.**

3. In small groups, ask members to share their thoughts on what they consider to be their boundaries of responsibility. For example, do female and male participants have similar responsibilities in times of crisis? Is the intervention of a male or female more appropriate in certain circumstances? Where do they feel their responsibilities should end? When does safety become paramount? Do the expectations of management coincide with these boundaries? The idea is to work towards identifying the moment at which the staff will push their 'fire alarm button'. **10 min.**

4. Each small group now agrees and feeds back a short report. **5 min.**

5. Using the information gathered in Stages 1 and 3, each group should now start work on an emergency fire drill. There should be consensus about the point at which they would push the alarm button. This is vital for the confidence of every individual, as well as for the efficient implementation of the measures. In a large group, members should list the order of events.

    Under each event the relevant details should be worked out: When does it happen? Who decides? Who does what? Who supports whom? What specific responsibilities do people have? What specific support is needed? Are there any back-up procedures if things go wrong? When would outside help be called for? **15 min.**

6. Once the overall strategy has been worked out, small working groups should be formed. Every group should be asked to explore a certain stage in the proceedings. For example, one group might work on the question of who should intervene in a crisis situation. How do you decide which staff are the most appropriate? In formulating their strategy, participants should, of course, draw on their own experiences of effective and ineffective intervention. **10 min.**

7. The groups feed back short reports to the whole group. **5 min.**

Feedback and discussion

What further work needs to be done? What action still needs to be taken? What staff training will this entail? Do participants feel safer and more secure for having gone through this process? Have they found any other value in the process? **5 min.**

Notes

The drill could be ordered in various ways. One way would be to have the stages defined in one column, the specific action to be taken in another, the specific person in another and in the last column any supportive action that would be taking place at each stage. Participants could use simulated situations to practise tactics, to gain clarity about procedures and to gain confidence. In the workplace, it is a good idea to involve young people in this kind of preparation and rehearsal. The drill is more likely to work – and less likely ever to be needed – if everyone has a share of the responsibility for it.

Skills

Teamwork. Support. Observation. Communication. Negotiation. Training. Planning. Clarity.

Exercise 6.11 Support Yourself

Time: 40 min.

Description

An individual and group exercise looking at ways in which participants can support themselves and the tools they will need for doing so.

Aims

To anticipate difficulties that participants are likely to face when they attempt to apply what they have learned from this course. To establish areas over which participants can take control and to develop a structure for supporting their aims.

Directions

1. Wordstorm all the areas of difficulty that participants are likely to face when they try to incorporate the ideas that they have been exploring into their work. Include difficulties from outside (such as structures within the workplace) and difficulties that participants might face personally (controlling their own anger, perhaps, or becoming more assertive with a particular person).   **5 min.**

2. Wordstorm the word 'support'. What does support mean to the participants? How can they support themselves so that they don't give up when faced with difficulties? **5 min.**

3. Divide participants into small groups to address the question of how each person can help themselves to stick to an ideal or commitment at difficult times, that is, how they can support themselves. Refer them to recent experiences such as failure to meet a deadline or difficulty in keeping a commitment to saving money. (At the end of the exercise is a suggested personal support structure for keeping on course when we feel we have failed in some way or mistakes have been made. It is discussed further in the notes.) **20 min.**

Feedback and discussion

Ask participants the following questions: What do you usually feel when you have failed or made a mistake? What is the effect of taking responsibility rather than making excuses? What is difficult about it? In what ways does taking responsibility for mistakes and 'failures' give you support? How will you know that your personal support structures are intact and working? What will you do to mend them when they are not? What value do they have? What is the difference between taking responsibility and shouldering the blame?   **10 min.**

Notes

Taking responsibility for mistakes and failures is a way of reclaiming personal power, instead of handing it over to excuses and explanations. We keep it within our power to change things or to make sure that the mistake is not made again. Taking responsibility is a very different act from 'shouldering the blame', which holds the person in the role of a victim. It is an act of self-empowerment. We may not have had control over what happened, but we can take control over how it affects us and how we deal with it.

Mistakes and failures happen only because a commitment has been made or when something that has been tried has not worked. Making commitments and taking responsibility for them can be empowering for the individual. Apportioning blame, finding fault or making excuses has the opposite effect. Do we really want to give our circumstances such power over our lives?

Skills

Imagination. Analysis. Creative thinking.

Support structure

- Acknowledge what you have done.

- Accept responsibility for it.

- Clean up what you have done (that is, have any necessary conversations, clean up the mess).

- See what you can do to make sure it will not happen again.

Exercise 6.12 Reparation, Recovery and Gain

Time: 60 min.

Description

An exercise to explore the concepts of recovery and reparation and to develop some practical strategies for the workplace.

Aims

To explore methods for staff recovery and reparation after a traumatic event in the workplace. To gain an understanding of the effects of traumatic events on the individual as well as within a staff group. To share how recovery and reparation methods could be used with young people themselves. To decide on practical ways of applying these methods.

Directions

1. Wordstorm the words 'reparation' and 'recovery' with the whole group. Write up all comments. **5 min.**

2. In small groups, invite participants to talk about any traumatic event they have experienced in the workplace. Ask them to focus on the effects it had on them afterwards: the personal effects; the effects on their work; the effects on their relationships with colleagues, management and young people; and the effect it had on their lives outside work. **15 min.**

3. In the large group, ask small groups to feed back all the ideas they shared, ideally summarised into single words or short phrases. **5 min.**

4. Again in small groups, ask participants to focus on the methods of recovery that they used or might have used. Have any of them managed to heal the rift with the other party? If so, how? If methods were tried and failed, why did they not work? **10 min.**

5. In the large group, get the small groups to report back on recovery and reparation strategies. The whole group could then look at practical methods by which staff members could receive support and other assistance, such as time off, counselling or compensation. What help is needed from outside? What help can be given by colleagues? What strategies could be implemented with young people and practised to their benefit? Practical guidelines could now be drawn up, with specific reference to the workplace. **15 min.**

Feedback and discussion

What do participants feel they have gained from this exploration? What practical strategies have they formulated? What pleases them about the agreed plan of action? What further exploration would make them feel more secure and positive about their working environment? **10 min.**

Notes

In this exercise we are putting the subject of recovery and reparation on the agenda. It is important to emphasise the possibility of positive gain through this process. New strengths and new confidence can be built. Difficult and traumatic experiences can be put to constructive use. Like unresolved conflict, every crisis has a cost. Working on reparation and recovery is a way of finding the gains.

Skills

Communication. Sharing. Analysis. Planning.

Chapter 7
Mediation and Action for Change
Towards Community Action

Just as we are all fuel for fires that can burn and destroy, so are we fuel for fires that can light our lives and warm our hearts. A spark lands on dry tinder and starts off the fire. It spreads and becomes a blaze. The blaze rejuvenates the ageing soil and offers us possibilities of new growth. It is a bright beacon. The flames dance with energy and opportunity.

The fire analogy can represent cooperation and creation as well as conflict and destruction:

The fuel The people, as before, who live and work with each other.

The spark A raw issue brings a flash of new insight to a community. It is taken up by the livewire, who initiates a plan to bring about change.

Smouldering The idea is mulled over and talked about. It is picked up by others, who persist in encouraging others still to think about it and to respond.

Fanning the flames Strength is gathered when new people join in who have skills in solving problems. They give life to the slow-burning fire.

Stoking the fire Consolidating what has been gained, the advocates and the trail-blazers pile on encouragement and support for action.

The blaze Finally the stoked fire bursts into great flames. The beacon has been lit. It is a light that will not go out. It gives warmth, energy and inspiration.

The creative blaze is the work of livewires, initiators, persisters and peacemakers. They spark, smoulder, fan and stoke, as do the agitators and provokers of conflict. Their behaviour is regenerative. The blaze brings new challenges, with change and rejuvenation. We are all fuel; we are all potential beacon-builders.

This chapter explores the process of mediation and other creative approaches to bringing about change through social action.

Full training to be a mediator is outside the scope and timeframe of this course, but this section offers practice in key mediation skills and examines their application in the heat of the moment.

Focus

Mediation; exploring intervention in situations of intense conflict; exploring nonviolent options; exploring strategies for social change.

Key concepts

Mediation; non-violence; intervention; taking sides; social change.

Key questions

Can we use the ideas and principles of mediation in situations of challenge? What do we mean by the concept of neutrality? When might we take sides in a conflict? What can I do as an individual to bring about social change? What are the non-violent options available to us? Do different crises require different intervention strategies?

Mediation and Action for Change

7.1	Introduction to Mediation	45 min.
7.2	Questioning	30 min.
7.3	Facts and Feelings	30 min.
7.4	Behind the Scenes	35 min.
7.5	Words Unheard	35 min.
7.6	Acting Impartially	45 min.
7.7	Mediation in the Moment	50 min.
7.8	The Boxing Ring	75 min.
7.9	Conflict in Action: Intervention for Change	130 min.
7.10	Taking Sides	45 min.
7.11	Non-violent Action	60 min.
7.12	Action for Change	130 min.

Exercise 7.1 Introduction to Mediation

Time: 45 min.

Description

A whole-group exercise to explore the core concepts of mediation.

Aims

To distinguish mediation and the role of a mediator from other methods of responding to conflict. To identify the key philosophies and principles behind mediation. To highlight the main steps of the mediation process.

Directions

1. Prepare three pieces of flipchart paper headed 'What is mediation and how does it work?', 'What are some of the philosophies and principles that underpin mediation?' and 'Why is mediation different from other methods of resolving conflict?' respectively. Space the sheets as far apart as possible on the walls. **2 min.**

2. Divide the participants into three groups. Give each group a different coloured pen and ask them to appoint a recorder. Each group chooses a place to start. They have three minutes at their first station to record their answers to the question, using the principles of a wordstorm. **5 min.**

3. Call time and move each group on to the next sheet, taking their pen with them. They need to read the contributions of the previous group and add any additional ideas of their own. Repeat this with the third sheet. **6 min.**

4. Bring participants and flipchart sheets back to the main group. Take participants through Handouts 1, 2, and 3 for Exercise 7.1. **10 min.**

5. A mediator is often called a third party, which means someone who is not involved in the conflict, that is, they are not a party to the situation. Ask participants to wordstorm other third-party roles they are familiar with, for example, referee, judge, parent, boss. Ask them to identify who has control of the outcome in each situation. **5 min.**

6. Take participants through Handout 4 for Exercise 7.1. **5 min.**

Feedback and discussion

Allow a little time for questions about mediation and the mediation process – its functions, its benefits, its uses, its difficulties – and give examples of successful mediation processes. **12 min.**

Notes

You can develop this exercise further by exploring in more detail why mediators do not make suggestions or tell people what to do. The following questions might be used: In mediation, it can be hard not to make suggestions. Why do you think that is? What's it like when someone gives you advice or tells you what to do? How do you react? Why is it not appropriate in mediation to give advice?

This concept may be challenging for mediators who, having heard both sides of a story, can think they are in a good place to offer advice. The key to mediation is for the parties to find ways to resolve the problems for themselves.

Skills

Sharing ideas. Discussion. Clarification.

Handout 1 for Exercise 7.1

Introduction to Mediation

Mediation is a way of resolving conflict where two parties come together voluntarily with the mediators to talk through their conflict and find their own solutions. The mediators are impartial or neutral (that is, they do not take sides); they take the parties through a step-by-step process which helps them explore what has happened and decide what to do next.

The **philosophies behind mediation** are that:

- positive outcomes can come from conflict
- there are two sides to every story (at least)
- the parties in a conflict are the best people to resolve it
- there are solutions that meet the needs of both parties in a conflict situation.

The **key principles of mediation** are that:

- participation is voluntary
- the focus is on the problem, not the people
- the focus is on the future
- parties agree to their own solutions
- the focus is on win-win
- the process is confidential.

Mediation differs from other conflict resolution processes because the parties decide the outcome of the conflict and the mediators do not have the power to enforce any decisions.

Negotiation

The parties or their representatives work out an agreement or contract between themselves.

Conciliation

Conciliation is very similar to mediation. The role of the conciliator is to help the parties resolve the dispute for themselves. The terms 'mediation' and 'conciliation' have been used interchangeably.

Arbitration

Two parties agree on the appointment of an arbitrator, who consults the parties and makes a judgement which is often binding on the parties.

Litigation

The parties take their dispute through the legal process. The dispute will be settled by the judge according to the rule of law.

Handout 2 for Exercise 7.1

The mediation process

PRE-MEETING WITH PARTY 1	PRE-MEETING WITH PARTY 2
• Hear their account.	• Hear their account.
• Explain mediation.	• Explain mediation.
• Explore options.	• Explore options.

If both parties agree

JOINT MEETING

- introduction

- facts (what has happened)

- feelings (how they have been affected by what has happened)

- identifying issues (what needs to be resolved)

- fantasies (ideas for resolving the situation)

- future (deciding the way ahead).

Handout 3 for Exercise 7.1

Mediation language

Confidentiality

What people say in mediation is not spoken about outside the room – this also applies to the mediators who will only break that confidence if parties talk about harming others or themselves.

Impartial

The mediators' role is not to take the side of either party but to act neutrally.

Mediation process

The different stages of mediation that the mediators take the parties through. This includes the pre-meetings and the joint meeting.

Party

The parties are the people involved in the conflict. In mediation the parties are referred to as Party One – generally the person who brought the conflict to mediation – and Party Two.

Third party

The mediators are often referred to as the third party, which means that they are not part of the conflict. Their job is to help the people in conflict resolve the situation.

Voluntariness

The parties must choose to take part in mediation for themselves and not be made to take part.

Win-win

The focus in mediation is on finding solutions that both parties are happy with – as opposed to win-lose where one party gets what they want and the other does not.

Handout 4 for Exercise 7.1

The role of the mediator

The **role of a mediator** is to:

- be responsible for the process but not the content of the meetings
- help people communicate with each other
- act as a bridge between parties
- be fair and balance the needs of each party.

It is **not** to:

- judge (say who is right or wrong)
- blame (say what someone should or should not have done)
- give advice, opinions or suggestions
- be an authority and lay down the law (say what to do)
- befriend
- be a counsellor.

Mediator skills:

- active listening
- summarising
- separating facts and feelings
- being empathetic
- questioning
- acting impartially
- reframing
- co-working
- seeing both perspectives
- staying calm and centred.

Exercise 7.2 Questioning

Time: 30 min.

Description

An individual and paired exercise to explore the use of different types of questions.

Aims

To recognise the impact of different questions on the speaker. To explore using questions for specific intentions.

Directions

1. Individually, participants should identify some general questions they might ask to help someone gain greater understanding of a particular problem. Ask them to make a list of these questions. **4 min.**

2. Ask participants to get into pairs. One person will think of a problem that they are currently experiencing. The other person will ask them five questions from their list, noting the effect of each question; for example, does it encourage or close down the speaker? **8 min.**

3. Swap roles and repeat the exercise. **8 min.**

Feedback and discussion

What did the participants notice about the effect of their questions? Which questions were more useful in drawing out information? Which questions were more useful in getting specific details about the situations? Which questions were more useful for focusing on the future? **10 min.**

Notes

Questioning is a key skill for mediators. Mediators need to be familiar with open questions (those that open up discussion and cannot be answered with one word), which are used to encourage the sharing of information and broaden the discussion, and closed questions (those which have a yes/no or one-word answer), which are used to get specific information or to clarify what was said. A third type of question – the 'What if…?' question – helps to focus on the future and what they would like to happen, and can be useful for reality testing. Encourage the participants to make a note of useful questions as they hear them so they can build up a list to refer back to.

Skills

Listening. Questioning. Analysis.

Exercise 7.3 Facts and Feelings

Time: 30 min.

Description

An exercise in small groups practising separating facts from feelings.

Aims

To distinguish between facts and feelings. To practise listening for facts and feelings in conflict. To practise feedback skills.

Directions

1. Divide the participants into groups of three. Ask each participant to identify a personal conflict they feel comfortable sharing with others which is not too upsetting. **5 min.**

2. One participant in each group talks for three minutes about their conflict whilst the other two participants listen. One participant is listening for the facts of the story, and the other is listening for the feelings. After three minutes the listeners feed back, in turn, the facts and then the feelings that they heard being expressed. Allow two minutes for the feedback and a further minute for a quick review of the feedback. **6 min.**

3. Repeat with each participant telling their story and hearing back the facts and the feelings. **12 min.**

Feedback and discussion

What is helpful about separating out the facts from the feelings in this way? How might it be a helpful skill in mediation? **7 min.**

Notes

Being able to separate out facts and feelings is an important skill in mediation. Acknowledging someone's feelings in a conflict situation can be just as important as dealing with the facts of the conflict. Helping people to acknowledge the strong feelings they have in an instance of conflict can mean that they are more able to focus on finding solutions.

Skills

Listening. Separating facts and feelings. Summarising.

Exercise 7.4 Behind the Scenes

Time: 35 min.

Description

A paired exercise to explore both sides of a conflict and identify areas of common ground.

Aims

To identify what underpins a conflict situation from the perspective of each party. To explore areas of common ground between conflicting parties.

Directions

1. Ask participants to wordstorm conflict situations that might arise in their work situations in which they are a third party. Write these ideas on the flipchart.   **5 min.**

2. Ask participants to get into pairs and to pick one scenario from the list that is relevant or interesting to them. Give each pair a piece of flipchart paper and ask them to divide the sheet into quarters. On either side of the top half of the page, they should record the needs of each party. On either side of the bottom half of the page they should record the fears of each party as they perceive them.   **10 min.**

3. Ask them to compare the needs and fears of each party, looking for areas of common ground and ways of framing the problem in neutral terms.   **10 min.**

Feedback and discussion

Has exploring what lies behind a conflict given you a greater understanding of the situation? Has it enabled you to see any areas of common ground? Are you able to frame the conflict in neutral terms?   **10 min.**

Notes

This exercise brings together the learning from Exercises 7.3, Facts and Feelings, and 6.5, Positions, Interests, Needs, so participants can see how these concepts work in a conflict situation. It can be used as an exercise in its own right or as a lead-in to Exercises 7.5, Words Unheard, and 7.8, The Boxing Ring.

Skills

Imagination. Observation. Analysis.

Exercise 7.5 Words Unheard

Time: 35 min.

Description

A paired listening exercise to explore what underlies opposing points of view.

Aims

To practise summarising as a way of checking that we are really listening to what someone is saying. To explore the challenges of listening when there is disagreement.

Directions

1. In the whole group, wordstorm some broad societal issues on which participants might disagree; for example, political issues, environmental concerns, the ban on foxhunting, etc. Try to get a good list for people to choose from. **5 min.**

2. Ask participants to get into pairs and pick a topic from the list on which they disagree – if they cannot find something they truly disagree on, they need to find a topic where they can take opposing views. **5 min.**

3. Each pair should now decide who is A and who is B. Explain how the exercise works: A speaks first, putting forward their side of the argument. A has two minutes, during which B listens silently. When A has finished, B summarises what A has said. When A is happy with the summary, B then has two minutes to give the counter-argument to A. A will listen silently and then give a summary of what B has said to B's satisfaction. After the summary, A then continues putting forward their point of view. A and B should repeat this process three or four times – it is important that neither party speak without summarising what the other has said first. It can be helpful to write up the instructions on the flipchart. **15 min.**

Feedback and discussion

Is it hard to listen to someone you disagree with? Why? What happens to your listening? What did the structured summarising create? **10 min.**

Notes

Participants should have gained a greater understanding of the other's perspective and even identified some areas of common ground despite their opposing positions. This is a very structured exercise but it can very effectively mirror what happens in the mediation process if participants follow the steps carefully. It is often hard for parties in conflict to listen to each other because of the intensity of their emotions; it is the mediator's role to summarise what parties are saying in a way that makes it easier for each of them to hear what the other is saying. You can also use this exercise to illustrate the concept of positions, interests and needs by working through an example of the dialogue from one pair on the flipchart.

Skills

Concentrated listening. Summarising. Articulating a viewpoint.

Exercise 7.6 Acting Impartially

Time: 45 min.

Description

A small group tableau exercise to explore how our impartiality is challenged in conflict situations.

Aims

To explore how our biases may affect our role as a mediator. To identify strategies for minimising the effect of any biases.

Directions

1. Ask the participants to get into groups of two or three. Ask each group to pick one of the scenarios generated for Exercise 7.4, Behind the Scenes and to create a tableau of the conflict to show the wider group.   **5 min.**

2. As each scenario is shown, ask the wider group to say who they think is in the right and who is in the wrong in each scenario, whose side they are more likely to be on and why that is. Encourage the participants to identify some of the emotions they experience watching the scenarios.   **15 min.**

3. Ask the group to think about how these feelings might affect their behaviour if they were mediators in that situation, identifying what they might or might not do if they were partial towards or against someone. Record these behaviours on the flipchart.   **10 min.**

4. Encourage the group to draw up a checklist of strategies they could use to minimise any biases they might feel.   **5 min.**

Feedback and discussion

Were there any commonalities in the situations where participants felt biased towards or against one of the parties? What were some of the feelings and thoughts that came up in those situations? How can you minimise potential bias in conflict situations?   **10 min.**

Notes

A mediator's role is to act impartially, that is, not to take sides. In reality everyone has their own opinions, viewpoints and ideas, and most of us find some people easier to get on with than others. Mediators need to notice their thoughts and feelings so they can choose to put them aside and modify their behaviour if necessary.

Skills

Self-reflection. Honesty. Analysis.

Exercise 7.7 Mediation in the Moment

Time: 50 min.

Description

A small-group role-play exercise to explore using mediation skills and aspects of the mediation process in everyday work situations.

Aims

To develop and practise mediation skills in an active way and under pressure of time. To explore utilising aspects of the mediation process in the moment.

Directions

1. Take the participants through Handout for Exercise 7.7, Mediation in the Moment. This breaks down the mediators' tasks and identifies the skills used at each stage of the mediation process so that they can be used separately. **10 min.**

2. Divide participants into groups of four. Ask each group to identify several conflict situations in the workplace where they would need to intervene. Two members of the group will play the young people in the conflict situation, one person will be responsible for intervening and one person will provide support to the intervener. Whilst the young people develop their role-play, the intervener and supporter identify what steps they might take. **10 min.**

3. The young people should now start a conflict. The intervener should step in, using elements of the mediation process or mediation skills. **10 min.**

4. Participants swap roles and repeat the exercise. **10 min.**

Feedback and discussion

Which mediation skills and concepts were used? Which were effective and why? Which were not effective and why? What other strategies might have been useful? **10 min.**

Notes

Mediation is generally used as a formal process for resolving conflicts. However, many youth work situations are better resolved using more immediate and informal approaches; there are skills and elements of the mediation process that can be effective in the moment.

Skills

Role-play and improvisation. Creative thinking. Developing tactics.

Handout for Exercise 7.7

Mediation in the Moment

Stages of the mediation process	Concepts and skills	Transferable skills
Pre-Meeting	Talking through views of the situation	Listening
	Planning what they want from the meeting	Clarifying
	Think through how other party might respond	Summarising
	Getting permission to mediate	Questioning
Stage 1: Introduction	Setting Framework	Explaining concepts clearly
	Explaining purpose of meeting	
	Explaining role of mediator	
	Being clear about boundaries, behaviour, etc.	Explaining ground rules, getting agreement
Stages 2 & 3: Facts & Feelings	Each person gets space to describe the situation	Separating facts from feelings (Exercise 7.3)
		Separating positions, interests, needs (Exercise 6.5)
	Each person gets space to vent	Protecting uninterrupted time
	Summarise what each person has said	Listening and summarising
Stage 4: Identifying Issues	Venting	Allowing anger
	Impact of new information	Identifying issues
	Opportunity to respond/question	Naming what is happening
	Identifying issues and making them joint issues	Identifying common ground
	Agreeing and prioritising agenda	Facilitation skills
Stage 5: Fantasies	Working through issues one at a time	Skills as for Stage 4 plus
	Exploring options	Keeping the momentum going
	Keeping people future focused	
Stage 6: Future	Agreeing a way ahead	Skills as above plus
	Writing an agreement (balanced, fair, specific)	Reality checking
	Exploring future communication	
	Exploring 'what ifs'	

Exercise 7.8 The Boxing Ring

Time: 75 min.

Description

An structured role-play exercise to explore ways of responding to difficult or challenging situations.

Aims

To practise using the frameworks and tools shared in an active way and under pressure of time. To practise a method of supporting a participant in finding a response to a difficult or challenging situation.

Directions

1. This exercise offers the opportunity for some participants to try out new ways of dealing with a realistic challenge in a safe and contained environment. It uses the framework of a boxing ring. However, unlike in a real boxing ring, the intention here is to achieve a win-win solution rather than the more usual win-lose outcome of a boxing bout.

2. Ask participants to come up with examples of difficult situations they would like to find a response to. The group can then choose the situation they are most interested in working on. The boxing ring exercise involves a challenger versus an opponent. Ask for volunteers to take on these roles. Develop the scenario further with the group by asking:

   ◦ What is the challenge? It could, for example, be a conflict between a youth worker (the challenger) and a young person (the opponent) in the youth club over paying subscriptions.

   ◦ What is the outcome the challenger would like? (For example, the young person should either pay their subscription and come to the session or leave without causing a scene.)

   ◦ What is the first obstacle the challenger may meet? (For example, the young person may get angry when they are asked to pay their money.)

   ◦ What is the challenger's first strategy to overcome that obstacle? (For example, taking the young person to one side to talk to them rather than doing it in front of the others.)

   Record the answer on a flipchart. Create names for the challenger and the opponent; write these on sticky labels that they will wear during the exercise. **6 min**

3. Ask for two volunteers to act as coaches for the challenger. Their task will be to support the challenger, before the bout and during the breaks between rounds, to get the outcome that they want. They will provide feedback as to how the challenger is doing – what is and what is not working – as well as ideas and strategies to use in order for them to meet their goal. **2 min.**

4.   Ask for two volunteers to act as coaches for the opponent. The opponent's role is to provide a strong challenge so that the challenger will be emotionally and physically stretched. The coaches will give the opponent feedback – for example, whether the challenge presented is realistic, too easy or too difficult – as well as ideas and strategies to obstruct the challenger.   **2 min.**

5.   Ask for two or three volunteers to be journalists. Their task is to write an article on what they witness in the boxing ring in the style of a chosen publication. They may choose which paper they would like to write for. They will read back their stories after the role-play.   **2 min.**

6.   Give the challenger and opponent five minutes with their coaches to prepare for the role-play.   **5 min.**

7.   Mark out the boxing ring using chairs for the corners. There will be three rounds. The facilitator will act as the referee and they will call the beginning and end of each round. Allow approximately three minutes for a round and two minutes for coaching, although the referee will need to use their judgement about this, according to the action. For example, if the challenger is having too hard a time, the referee should call the end of a round so that the challenger can return to their corner to get support from their coaches. The referee can at any time call a 'freeze' in the action to give an instruction. Contrary to real life, there is a 'no physical contact' rule in the boxing ring.   **2 min.**

8.   Call the first round. The challenger and opponent enter the ring and the bout begins. The coaches stay outside of the ring in their respective 'corners' and closely observe the performance of their partners. They may not call out during the rounds. Call the end of the round when you think a good exchange has taken place.   **3 min.**

9.   In the break, the coaches can give their feedback and some quick advice as to the way forward in the next round.   **5 min.**

10.   Call the next round and let the challenge continue. The challenger and opponent try to follow the advice of their coaches as well as trying to respond to all the tactics of their opponent.   **3 min.**

11.   Call the next break. The challenger and opponent return to their corners and the coaches resume their duties. Call the final round, which will run until an end result is achieved; ideally this will be the challenger's desired outcome or somewhere along that spectrum from the original challenge.   **5 min.**

12.   Bring everyone back together in the large group to de-role the players (see 'Guidance for Trainers' for notes on de-roling). Start first with the challenger and opponent, then the coaches, observers and journalists.   **10 min.**

13.   Ask participants to share back skills or qualities they observed that worked in the exercise, for example, 'She listened and remained calm'.   **10 min.**

14.   Ask the journalists to read their stories. Give them a round of applause.   **10 min.**

Feedback and discussion

What is the value of having a chance to practise your responses in a tough situation? What becomes available to you if you prepare yourself before having to face a difficult situation? What becomes available to you if you create and receive a support system for yourself? What support worked in this exercise? What support didn't work? What was it like giving support to others? What was it like receiving support from others? **10 min.**

Notes

The use of a metaphorical boxing ring provides a clearly defined space in which the dispute can take place. It also provides a clear structure – the use of the 'referee', of 'corners', of 'coaches' and of rules and timekeeping. It also provides a sense of urgency and action. The conflict resolution techniques being practised obviously bear no resemblance to the win-at-all-costs violence of a boxing bout.

If there is time, give a few participants an opportunity to take their specific challenge into the ring. It is important to acknowledge the positive skills and qualities that were noticeable and utilised in each of the challengers' role-plays; participants need to experience what becomes available to them when they use a specific skill or display a certain quality. It is useful also to highlight the techniques used by each of the opponents in order to undermine, manipulate and hook the challenger. By giving these a name they will be easier to recognise and deal with in future.

This exercise can be used effectively with groups of young people, for example, to practise dealing with a red flag more constructively or to practise stepping back from a potentially violent confrontation. It can also be used for young people to explore their relationships with their peers. For example, the challenger could be rehearsing a situation where one of their friends is trying to persuade them to back them up in a fight or a crime.

Skills

Role-play and improvisation. Listening and observation. Decision-making. Developing tactics. Taking instructions. Using advice.

Exercise 7.9 Conflict in Action:
Intervention for Change

Time: 130 min.

Description

An exercise using role-play to enact the progression of a particular conflict, with the purpose of exploring how intervention could have prevented a destructive or negative outcome.

Aims

To explore the fire analogy as a practical tool in conflict resolution. To look at all the different stages in a conflict where positive intervention is possible. To see how the nature of the intervention will differ depending on the stage of the conflict.

Directions

1. Making use of the table entitled 'Fire: conflict and change' (see p.15) and the 'Fire and conflict' illustration at the beginning of the book, remind the participants of the stages of the fire analogy. Ask every participant to think of a conflict that they have been involved in, or one that they are very familiar with. They should ideally choose one that developed over a period of time, with fairly clear points of progression, not a conflict that flared up quickly and was all over in a couple of minutes. Each participant will attempt to subdivide the stages of their conflict under each of the headings of the fire analogy. They can skip a stage if it is not appropriate. **15 min.**

2. This work can be shared by the large group or, if the group is too large, in smaller groups of four or five members. Each small group should then choose one of their members' conflicts to dramatise and share with the larger group. **15 min.**

3. During the preparation the participants need to consider all the points at which intervention could be successful and which different interventions may be appropriate at different stages. (A conflict which has reached the blazing stage, for instance, will require more radical forms of intervention than a smouldering situation.) **30 min.**

4. The groups show back their role-plays. (If there is only one large group, the facilitators can function as the audience.) They then select one scene or section and ask the audience for suggestions as to how one character could intervene to make a positive contribution to the possible resolution of the conflict. The scene is replayed. The audience can call 'freeze' at any point and make a suggestion for one of the characters to try out. If the member playing that part is not sure how to enact the suggestion, the person who made the suggestion could take over the role temporarily and try it out. In this way various ideas can be rehearsed.

    All the groups share their work in this way. They can also reflect afterwards on all the other thoughts they had regarding possible interventions at other stages of the conflict. **55 min.**

Feedback and discussion

What choices did the various characters have? Were the moments of escalation clear? What were the moments at which alternative action could have changed the situation? How did the fire analogy provide a useful focus for the study of the development of the conflict? Could participants suggest improvements to the analogy? Could they develop an analogy of their own?

15 min.

Notes

Using the fire analogy in this way can empower people to analyse, understand and take control of their own disputes. Depending on the kinds of conflicts you are working with it might be interesting to explore how the energy of a potentially destructive conflict might be captured and harnessed to bring about positive change.

Skills

Role-play. Analysis. Group devising. Interaction.

Exercise 7.10 Taking Sides

Time: 45 min.

Description

A small group tableau exercise to explore the issue of taking sides in community conflicts.

Aims

To explore the concept of neutrality in more complex situations. To explore the concept of taking sides.

Directions

1. Divide participants into small groups of four or five. Ask each group to think of examples of conflicts happening in their communities that they have some knowledge of.

   Each group will select one community situation and create a group tableau that illustrates the core of the conflict. They should create a voiceover or narration to accompany the tableau which illustrates the causes of the conflict and its escalation. **15 min.**

2. The groups share back their tableaux. Participants focus on the possible roles of a third-party intervener in these situations, thinking particularly about whether or not it is possible to be neutral and what the advantages or disadvantages of being neutral might be. **20 min.**

Feedback and discussion

Have participants ever taken sides in a community conflict? How and why did they do this? Is it possible to take a neutral stance? Is it possible to take sides without supporting the use of violence? **10 min.**

Notes

Exercise 7.6, Acting Impartially, explored the concept of impartiality in mediation. This exercise considers whether it is possible to be neutral in more complex situations.

Many models of peacemaking have a neutral intervener bringing together the two sides to the conflict to seek a peaceful resolution. However, this model may ignore or hide the structural injustices in society, where groups are being oppressed or exploited and where to be neutral would mean colluding with the oppressors. There is a difference between 'papering over the cracks' to create a temporary façade of peace and creating a fair and just society. What is important is to work towards peace without the use of violence.

Skills

Physical expression. Imagination. Communication and exploration. Self-reflection.

Exercise 7.11 Non-violent Action

Time: 60 min.

Description

A group exercise exploring what non-violent action means and drawing up steps for practical action.

Aims

To explore the notion of non-violent action. To share different options available and examine a selection of options in detail. To rehearse strategies for action.

Directions

1. With the whole group, wordstorm the phrase 'non-violent action'. What kind of immediate responses does the term evoke? Divide into three groups to explore the following three areas: (1) the methods of protest and persuasion; (2) the methods of non-cooperation; and (3) the methods of intervention. These are three distinct approaches to non-violent action, in ascending order of intensity and commitment.   **5 min.**

2. Ask the small groups to think of all the ways of responding under their specific heading. You could help, if and when it seems appropriate, by supplying examples from the list on the Handout for Exercise 7.11, Non-violent Action.   **10 min.**

3. Each group should now prepare for a presentation to the other groups. They should select some examples and, by using a combination of tableaux, props, movement, voices and narration, dramatically present their chosen ideas to the big group.   **15 min.**

4. A smaller number of examples can then be further selected from those that have been presented. These could be, for example, mass petition, march, consumer boycott, sit-down, alternative transport.

    Each group is asked to choose one of these to explore in depth – for example, a mass petition. How would they organise it? What are the first steps to take? What tasks will be required? How will supporters be recruited? What financial resources are needed and how will they be raised? These explorations can be shared at the end with the larger group.   **20 min.**

Feedback and discussion

What have participants' own experiences been in adopting this kind of action? What is the value of non-violence? What is the impact on others? What did the exercise reveal?   **10 min.**

Notes

It is interesting to consider that non-violent action can take place on a psychological, physical, social, economic or political level. You could ask participants to try grouping their examples under these headings and consider the potency and impact of each approach. Gene Sharp (1973) listed 198 methods of non-violent action. Details of his work can be found in the references.

A handout of quotations on non-violence would be useful as a warm-up and introduction to this section. You could either prepare a sheet or encourage the group to develop its own collection.

Skills

Interaction. Communication. Planning.

Handout for Exercise 7.11

Non-violent Action

Protest and persuasion

speeches … statements … letters … online or handwritten petitions … slogans … symbols … banners … posters … the media … leaflets and pamphlets … lobbies … pickets … symbolic actions … flags … colours … wearing symbols … prayer … changing names … vigils … drama … street theatre … music and songs … marches … silence … mock funerals … renouncing honours … turning your back

Non-cooperation

boycotts … strikes … disobedience … stay-at-homes … disappearance … withholding rent … lock-out … withdrawal of money … non-payment … embargoes … withdrawal from institutions … refusal to disperse … sit-downs … selective lawbreaking … deliberate inefficiency … tax refusals … non consumption of boycotted goods

Intervention

fasting … harassment … obstruction … sabotage … raids … occupations … camps … blockades … dismantling reverse strikes … alternative markets, transport, institutions, systems … seeking imprisonment … overloading the administrative systems … public scrutiny of oppressors … setting up parallel governments

Exercise 7.12 Action for Change

Time: 130 min.

Description

Tableau work in small groups charting the progression of actions in bringing about social change.

Aims

To analyse the stages involved in bringing about change. To highlight the social change we want to see. To determine the different stages for getting there.

Directions

1. Remind the group of the stages of the fire analogy (Exercise 7.9, Conflict in Action: Intervention for Change) and the kind of behaviours that characterise each stage of a conflict. In this course we have used the image of fire to help us see conflict both as a potential danger and a possible opportunity for change and creativity. We are now going to look at the blaze as something we welcome; as a fire which signifies a change we are seeking. Wordstorm campaigns for change which the group believes have succeeded in their aims.   **10 min.**

2. Working in small groups, ask the participants to identify the blaze or change they would like to see. They should spend some time sharing their ideas, then choose one idea to work on. This could be something that involves the whole community, such as an end to homelessness; or it might be something that focuses on our immediate community, such as relieving the effects of homelessness on local young people. Whatever they choose becomes the blaze they will be working on.   **20 min.**

3. Ask the participants to take each stage of the fire analogy, starting with the fuel, and assess what resources and skills they have at each stage. What must be achieved at each stage? What results are needed before they can move on? What are the key issues and aims of each stage? What action will be involved?   **20 min.**

4. Ask the groups to create a series of tableaux summing up the core action at each stage. They should aim to include the practicalities, the kind of behaviour and the people who will be involved.   **20 min.**

5. Ask each group to show back their tableaux work. You can use the following questions: Who is in the tableau? What are they doing? What effect is it having? What effect will it have? What skills and resources are needed at this stage? What skills and resources are being used? What will the side-effects (positive and negative) of this be? What support do people have at this stage? What kind of difficulties will there be? Who or what will be a hindrance? How will that hindrance be countered?   **45 min.**

Feedback and discussion

What have participants gained from this exercise? What are their practical ideas for effecting social change? How does the fire analogy help us to understand the process of change?

15 min.

Notes

Just as the fire analogy was used to facilitate analysis of conflict and its escalation, so it can be used to analyse a campaign or an action to bring about positive change. (To illustrate this, you can copy and hand out the case study on p.200.) The analogy can also help campaigners to understand the process on which they are embarking, and to plan their campaign successfully. However, it is also important for participants to recognise that any campaign is likely to be met with opposition.

Skills

Physical expression. Interaction. Analysis. Group strategies.

Handout for Exercise 7.12

Action for Change

Bringing about social change

The fuel

The residents of a block of flats on Princess Street come from a variety of cultural and ethnic origins. They blame each other's children for smoking, drinking, making noise and obstructing the stairwells and corridors in the block at night. Everyone has someone, or some group, to blame. There is a high degree of antagonism in the block.

The spark

One family who is fed up with the backbiting decides to initiate positive change and work towards a supportive, secure community.

Smouldering

The family organises a meeting with two like-minded residents. Together these people plan the action they will take.

Fanning the flames

They gather help and support from others. Between them they visit every flat in the block and talk to the residents about their fears, anxieties, grievances and needs. They hear from all the residents, not just the vocal few.

Stoking the fire

Many of the residents feel that their concerns are now being heard and want to be involved in seeing that they get addressed. They no longer feel isolated. A Residents' Association is set up, meeting the need for a central body which will address the grievances and fears of the residents including young people, who say that there is nowhere else to go to meet together.

The blaze

The Residents' Association is up and running. The regular meetings are attended by large numbers of residents. Plans for setting up a local mediation and peer mediation scheme for young people are under way. The option of using a vacant flat as a community venue for all ages is explored. The date for a 'Big Lunch' party for the whole block has been set for June.

Notes

The key to the success of this campaign was that the initiators listened to the needs and fears of all the residents, even those who had been involved in creating the unrest and had originally shown no evidence of wanting to change the situation cooperatively.

As soon as people began to appreciate that no one was telling them how to behave, they gradually became open to listening to what other residents were feeling. The difficulties came to be seen as belonging to the whole community, not merely to one or another group within it, and could therefore be addressed constructively by everyone.

Guidance for Trainers
Facilitating Change, Conflict, Growth

Our experience is that running an intensive 'Playing with Fire' course can be as challenging and confronting for the trainers as it is for the participants. Just as participants go on a journey of self-discovery and growth, so do the training team. It is Leap's premise that in order to deliver this work you need to *be* this work. Participants need to see in you a role-model, a leader, a facilitator, a guide and a fellow traveller. Participants will challenge you, inspire you and take you to your learning edge. They will test your knowledge, your ability to hold tough conversations, to navigate surely through tricky terrain. This is just as it should be. Developing as a trainer in confronting conflict is about learning concepts and techniques, but it is also about developing practical skills, trying new ways of thinking and doing, getting into deep water (and getting out again safely), setting out into the unknown and taking leaps of courage. This is all so that you can work more effectively with young people who are facing challenges for a host of reasons, sometimes just because they are young and trying things out for the first time.

Focus

Creating a supportive learning environment; course rituals and activities; the use of drama and role-play; working with conflict and challenge.

Creating a supportive learning environment

There are many challenges for the facilitator of a sustained piece of group work like 'Playing with Fire'. Creating a safe learning environment in which people feel able to challenge and support each other is crucial.

This section covers the elements we suggest are required to establish that environment. We suggest you cover these in the first two days of the programme.

Introductions

It is commonly said that first impressions are important and in the first 10 to 15 minutes of the first session participants will be experiencing a whole range of mixed feelings; they will be nervous, excited, vulnerable and scared, and will be looking at you as a facilitator and wondering how much they can rely on you to create the safe learning environment they will need.

You will have to think through and carefully plan your introduction with your co-trainer. What will you say about yourselves? How will you describe the programme and its aspirations? What will participants need to know about the kinds of activities that they will be engaged in? How will you make them feel welcome and comfortable? When and how will you ask participants to introduce themselves to the group? How will you use their introductions to get them to begin focusing on the subject in hand?

Expectations

Early on in the first day it will be beneficial to give participants an opportunity to work individually and in pairs on their expectations of the course, and then share these in the large group. You can use this as a way of clarifying the aims of the programme with participants, checking that their expectations are realistic and in line with the course content and process, and creating clarity around what the course will cover and – importantly – will not cover.

Group contract

There are many different ways of making a group contract. On a longer course like this it is a good idea to engage participants as much as possible in coming up with and owning their own group contract.

You could begin by asking them to spend some time thinking about the following questions:

What kinds of behaviours in a group lead me to shut up, shut down or get in the way of my learning?

What kinds of actions and behaviours would support the creation of a safe learning environment for all?

Participants can first share their responses with a partner and between them formulate some clear requests that they would like to make of the rest of the group regarding the kinds of actions and behaviours that would help them learn.

The trainer can then gather responses from the pairs and agree with the whole group an overall group contract for the programme. It is usual that the group contract will cover some or all of the following: contributing through speaking; listening and taking part; the use of mobile phones; agreeing expectations regarding time and punctuality; the boundaries of confidentiality.

Some common facilitation issues arising out of a group contract exercise are:

- the request that people 'respect each other'. There are a whole variety of interpretations of the word 'respect', and what might look like respect to one person looks like disrespect to another. Questions such as: 'What would that look like/sound like in the room?' support a more meaningful discussion about behaviours that are acceptable to the group

- the request that people are 'non-judgemental' towards one another. Useful questions to explore this request further might be: 'Can we really stop ourselves from making judgements?' 'If we could stop ourselves, would we want to?' 'What's important in this?' It is very difficult to stop ourselves from forming judgements and opinions of others; the important issue is what we do with them, that is, do we communicate them, critique them, dismiss others based on them, use them to challenge ourselves? Given that we do make judgements and have opinions what kind of behaviour do we want to see in this group towards others that will support a safe creative learning environment?

At the end of this exercise ask participants if you have their permission to support them in keeping to the contract.

On a programme such as this where some participants will have a level of familiarity with group processes and some may be trainers or facilitators themselves, you may also want to cover the following:

- Request that participants allow you to facilitate and allow themselves to participate, and notice when they are drawn into facilitating other group members or have the impulse to do so.

- Request that participants allow themselves to be fully on the course, that is, not making calls to work during breaks, not popping into the office before or after the course, and so on.

- Agree the level of challenge and support participants would like from other participants.

- Create an awareness of the relationship between feelings of comfort, discomfort and learning. For instance, receiving feedback on how we communicate or present ourselves can sometimes feel uncomfortable. However, that feedback might usefully facilitate our growth in terms of increasing our resources for working with conflict effectively. (See 'Praise, Criticism or Feedback?' on p.224.)

- Talk about levels of participation – the more you put into a course like this the more you will get from it.

Personal challenges/Goal setting

On the first or second day set aside time to ask participants what they would like the programme to help them improve or develop in terms of their own relationship to conflict and their work with young people.

Facilitate them in creating personal challenges or goals for themselves that are specific and demonstrable in the training room, for example, 'speaking up when I feel uncomfortable', 'listening when I have strong feelings or opinions' and also realistic and achievable during the period of training.

This gives them an additional and personal aim to work towards over the course.

When all participants have shared their personal challenge or goal in the large group we suggest that the facilitators then ask them for permission to give support in achieving their goals. Talk through what that might mean in terms of direct interventions, for example, asking questions, saying what you see, reflecting back to them and so on.

A good introduction to this is Exercise 1.5, Testing the Water.

Course rituals and activities

Leap trainers have trialled various methods of developing group trust and openness. The best of these have been adopted as regular activities that are used to help set up or frame the whole and/or parts of the day, and these are described below.

Clearings

Clearings are held each morning apart from the first. Each day can begin with a clearing. There are three main purposes to this activity:

- To allow some facilitated time for participants to reflect deeply on the course and to deepen their learning. Individual participants might use the clearing to reflect on their personal challenge, to share their experience of a particular exercise or activity from the day before or to offer an appreciation or affirmation of someone else in the group.

- To clear any leftover issues from the day before in terms of the group process that might interfere with someone continuing to learn. For example, a participant might use the clearing to ask that something be added to the group contract, to say if someone else's words or actions are affecting their learning, feelings of safety and so on.

- To allow facilitators to offer feedback to individuals or the group on personal challenges, issues they think may be affecting individual or group learning, or to deepen the learning around a piece of work from the previous day.

A well-facilitated clearing can be an excellent learning opportunity for the whole group in terms of seeing the frameworks and tools of the course applied in practice, especially to difficult and/or challenging moments of communication. They are opportunities for participants to *wander* and *wonder* in the pursuit of insights into their own and others' behaviour in conflict.

Clearings can last from half an hour to an hour, depending on how much there is to discuss and how confident and skilled you feel at facilitating this kind of conversation-based learning. If you do not feel confident at facilitating at this level keep the clearing to a maximum of half an hour.

SOME GUIDELINES AROUND WHAT CLEARINGS ARE AND ARE NOT

Clearings are:

> an inquiry into some or all of the following: conflict; our words and actions and the impact of them on others; what it means to take responsibility for our words and actions; our habits in conflict; why we do what we do when we feel uncomfortable, under attack, and so on; how hard it is to be affirmed and appreciated; the impact of some or all of the above on the young people we work with

Clearings are not:

> Q & A sessions with participants asking questions and facilitators giving the answers; group therapy; time for participants (or facilitators) to give lectures, offer advice or tell stories.

Clearings are held in the morning as it gives time for both participants and facilitators to absorb and reflect on overnight the experience of the previous day before speaking about it. In their trainer debrief at the end of each day trainers can select a couple of questions based on any issues that have come up during the sessions to start the clearing the following morning.

Gatherings

Gatherings can be used as a way of framing sessions or sections of the day.

They are large group go-rounds that collect and help bind the group together at the beginning or end of a session. The subject of a gathering can be frivolous or deep, depending on the need of the group or process at that particular point in the programme. Some favourite Leap examples are: 'if I were a kitchen implement I would be a...' and why; 'a colour I would be' and why; and 'someone I look up to' and why. Each participant speaks in turn, giving a brief response, going all the way round the circle.

Games

Games can serve a number of purposes in this kind of group work. They can be used as:

- icebreakers
- warm-ups
- lead-ins
- energy changers
- trust builders.

Examples of different games are given in the next section, 'Games and Group Discussion Techniques'.

Using quotations

Trainers use inspirational quotations in a range of different ways. Some use them as a way of introducing the focus or themes for the day. Others use them in the moment to illustrate a particular learning point that has arisen during a clearing or a feedback session. Most Leap trainers have collections of their favourite quotations!

Tender loving care (TLC) groups

This activity encourages the group to take practical responsibility for creating a pleasant, purposeful working environment. Participants are assigned to a different group for each block of training (for example, a weekend) and each group has a specific task to perform. The three groups are:

- the Timekeeping Group – they are responsible for reminding participants of the time so that everyone is back in the room ready to start on time after lunch and breaks
- the Games Group – they run games at the request of the trainers (though it is sensible as a trainer to have a game or an activity ready just in case)
- the Beauty and Order group – they are responsible for encouraging people to keep the workspaces clean, ordered and pleasant.

Find an enjoyable way of gathering people into their group each time. When you have a large number of participants these groups are particularly helpful in keeping the course running smoothly.

Go-round or whip-round

This can be an opportunity for participants to reflect briefly on an exercise, a session or the whole day. You can use this for different purposes according to need. It involves everyone responding to the same question. For example, you might ask everyone to give themselves a number indicating their energy level from 1 to 5, with 1 being low and 5 being high. You may ask everyone for one word that describes how they are feeling at the end of a session. Or at the end of the day you might ask participants to say one thing they are taking away from the day. It is a useful tool for the facilitators when they want to gauge quickly the mood, energy or learning of the group.

Paired sharing

Used when working with large groups, this is a useful tool – a way of participants sharing their different learning experiences following a small-group breakout session, as a way of focusing participants before a large-group feedback session or alternatively as a reflection aid at the end of the day.

Participants pair up with one other group member and take equal time to respond to a question or to reflect with each other on the day. Depending on the purpose they may then share back salient points to the large group.

Open reflection time

Participants speak or not according to whether or not they want to or have something to say. You may use open reflection time at the end of an exercise or at the end of the day, when it might follow a paired sharing.

End-of-day evaluation

It is important to ensure that the course content and delivery methods meet the participants' needs. One quick evaluation method would be to draw three lines on the flipchart. The first will evaluate 'Participation', the second 'Content' and the third 'Pace'. At either end of the first line write: 'Easy to participate' and 'Hard to participate'. At either end of the second line write: 'Useful' and 'Not useful'. At either end of the third write: 'Too fast' and 'Too slow'. Ask the participants to come up to the flipchart in groups and mark each line in accordance with their experience of the day. After everyone has given their feedback, give the group your interpretation of the result and ask for any further comments from the members.

Alternatively you could place three pieces of flipchart paper on the floor headed: 'What worked?' 'What didn't work?' and 'What could have been done differently?' respectively, and ask people to record their thoughts on the relevant sheets.

Buddy system

Participants choose or are assigned a buddy for the entire programme. They are invited to spend time with their buddy either at the beginning or the end of the day just to talk through any issues that are being raised by participating in the training, to offer support around personal challenges and so on.

Journal time

Provide participants with a journal at the beginning of the course. Encourage them to develop a reflective practice and to make a record of the journey of the course for future reference. A daily time slot allows an opportunity to record personal thoughts, observations, learning, quotes, exercises, anecdotes and progress from the course. Suggest that they may draw, doodle, write, create diagrams and flow charts, and provide materials to support the exercise.

The use of drama and role-play

Much of the experiential learning of this programme is through the use of drama and role-play techniques. These techniques enable the participants to rehearse a range of skills and strategies that they are developing. Practical rehearsal of this kind helps us move from 'head' knowledge to 'whole-self' knowledge, where feelings and emotions, the body and non-verbal communication can be engaged simultaneously with our thinking and reasoning. It is a holistic approach that argues that the development of rational and analytical learning must always be in partnership with an education of the feelings. After all, it is feelings that, in the end, are usually the provocation for most destructive and violent conflict.

Drama operates at normal life speed, whereas a lecture condenses and selects. Drama puts us at risk, draws from our unique well of life experience, engages the feminine and masculine dimensions in us all and brings the intuitive and spontaneous left-hand part of our brain into play alongside our linguistic and rational right-hand mode of being. We think and feel on our feet using drama just as we would in reality, yet there is an element of safety and distance, too, in playing a role.

The physical enactment of a difficult situation can be a more accurate way of assessing both the problem and its possible solutions. On reflection, we can examine our behaviour and our interactive style and be helped by others, and by our own insights, to try new and alternative responses.

There will usually be at least one participant on a training course who expresses a fear of role-play, sometimes because of poor experience of it on other training courses. Leap does not use role-play as a way of assessing people's practice or their acting abilities. In this manual it is used as a powerful technique to support the group task and learning process. However, role-play can provoke strong and sometimes unexpected emotions even when people are playing roles not directly related to their own experience, so it needs to be sensitively, skilfully and carefully facilitated.

Preparation

It is useful to make a distinction at this point. Some of the reluctance surrounding role-play is generated by the fear that acting is expected. This is true of dramatic characterisation, where the actor's task involves working on the truth of a *character*, but it is not true of task or skill-oriented role-play, which involves playing a *role* – an aspect, not the whole, of a character. It is helpful for facilitators to maintain clear boundaries between these two disciplines.

Be clear with participants about the purpose of a particular role-play, that is, remind them of the task you are all focused on, for example, the development of mediation skills, or developing strategies for dealing with aggressive behaviour from a young person.

Unless the role-play is very quick use labels in order to create a distinction between the role and the person playing it. Generally it is better to give people names rather than titles such as 'Obstructive' or 'Wind up', as it reminds participants that we are dealing with a real person rather than just the behaviour that we are struggling with. Removing a name label can also help the participant with de-roling at the end of the exercise.

It is important when working with drama and role-play techniques to pay attention to setting up the room so that participants can share back their work and everyone can see by creating a 'playing' area separate to the general seating. This will clearly define the workspace and also support participants in de-roling effectively. Ensuring that everyone receives applause will further support participation.

Role-play in action

There are a number of different ways of facilitating role-plays whilst they are going on. Before you begin you may want to agree how players show physical violence (for example, should they 'freeze' before the action?) and a method by which participants can stop the action if they feel uncomfortable or threatened in any way.

Intervention techniques

STOPPING AND PROCESSING

Ask role-players to come out of role for a short while. The facilitator then questions the players about what is going on. For example: What are your aims? Are you accomplishing them? If not, what is stopping you? This method is useful when the role-play is not working well, when it seems that the players have lost direction. By asking them questions you are not giving them your answers. The role-play is still in their hands. Your task is to encourage them to find their own answers to the difficulties they are facing.

HOT SEATING

The facilitator stops the role-play. The role-players remain in role while the facilitator questions them. Questions relate to the facilitator's aims – for a greater understanding of an individual the questions would be about how they feel, how they are being treated, what changes they would like from the situation, what are they hoping for, etc. This method is also useful when the role-play is stuck over an undisclosed piece of information. As facilitator you can question the characters in role and try to get that piece of information out into the open.

MODELLING AND DEMONSTRATING

The facilitator stops the role-play, moves in as one of the characters and shows another way of tackling the situation. This is a tricky method to use. It can result in role-players feeling undermined by the facilitator. It can, however, be used to good effect with an experienced group who know that this kind of intervention may occur. For the facilitator, it is an effective way of moving the role-play forward very quickly. To enhance group involvement, observers can also be given the opportunity to step in and change the action.

SUGGESTING AND DIRECTING

The facilitator stops the action, gives a direction and immediately moves out again. This is useful if the facilitator perceives that a player is straying from their given task. (It should be done sensitively, however, so as not to undermine their efforts.) It can also be used to speed up a process. The facilitator could give a direction which will force the group to come to a quick decision. (For example: 'The police are about to arrive – you have two minutes to come to a decision!') The facilitator can also use this method without stopping the action, by quietly whispering instructions into the ear of an individual. The participants will need to know in advance that this may happen.

All these methods require a ritual way of stopping action and restarting it. One commonly accepted way is to say 'freeze' or 'stop'. It is important to have an agreed word to use, known by everyone in advance of the exercise, so that stopping the action is clean and clear.

Processing role-play

HOT SEATING

The characters remain in role at the end of the role-play, and are asked questions to which they respond in character. Use this technique to find out more about what was going on in the role-play and how in-role characters felt about it.

DE-ROLING

De-roling is an important stage before moving on to feedback. It involves the individual players finishing off the role and officially coming out of it, with a very clear distinction between the role and the player, the 'mask' and the face. Give each character an opportunity to say anything else they need to in role. They then take off the in-role name tag and the facilitator welcomes the individual back into the group. You can also give the individual player an opportunity to say anything about or to the character they were playing. (The player speaks to an empty chair which represents the character they were playing.) This helps the player to come out of the role fully.

FEEDBACK

Questions for the group:
For example: Were the instructions clear? Was the facilitation helpful? What did you learn from the role play?

Questions for the facilitator:
For example: Did the group stick to the focus? Were individuals following instructions? Were the aims of the role-play met?

If there were major problems in the role-play, ask the role-players questions about their difficulties so they have an opportunity to find solutions. Remember, though, that de-roling must come before feedback and discussion. The two processes must not be confused. Participants should be allowed to leave their roles behind before being asked to discuss what did or did not work.

Using tableaux

This is a quick and active way of establishing the thoughts and feelings of group members without having to verbalise them. Tableaux (otherwise known as photographs, frozen images or statues) can be created individually, in pairs, in small groups or in a large group. A tableau might be created in response to a word – anger, for example. The participants would form their body into a shape that they felt corresponded to the theme. They might hold their fists up as if wanting to strike out at somebody. They might, on the other hand, present a more abstract physical image of angry thoughts and emotions. The facilitator might suggest that the participants form themselves into groups according to their interpretations of anger. All the aggressive images could combine to make a group tableau. If you combined the tableaux you would have a large tableau or photographic image to represent the entire group's response to the theme.

A development of this work is to ask all the frozen image participants to vocalise one thought or one word each. Participants can also be asked to move in slow motion from one frozen image to another – for example, from one interpretation of anger to another.

Another variation would be for participants to sculpt each other, or one participant could sculpt a whole group tableau around a specified theme or situation. (Sculpting involves one person moving another, or others, into a gesture or position by physically placing them in it – for example, raising their hand in the air – or explaining verbally what they want them to do, or demonstrating what they want. The person being sculpted holds the position as if they were a statue.)

Tableaux can be used to explore a wide range of themes or issues – family, community, school, employment, relationships, aggression, unity, division, and so forth. By creating a 'picture' participants can gain a different perspective on a situation or set of feelings and they can 'see' a story or situation differently. When using tableaux it is useful to remember the following points:

- Encourage people to think with their bodies rather than to use words. This will develop participants' aptitude for noticing and working with tableaux creatively as a tool. To this end it can be useful to encourage participants to stay on their feet rather than sit down when they are divided into smaller groups to sculpt images.

- If you are working with an individual participant's personal tableau ask someone else to swap in for the participant after seeing the images through the first time. This frees the participant to talk about the images they have created without having to hold the pose. It also allows them to see their pictures from outside and encourages them to reflect on the image more deeply and then be facilitated more easily through processing the learning gained from this process.

- It is good to remind participants only to make images they feel comfortable with, as tableaux can be used to represent painful or difficult events and feelings. Physical image work can be a powerful tool and can trigger memories and emotions for people even when they are not portraying themselves.

- A tableau can be physically hard to hold – especially when it is being processed. If this is the case ask participants to give themselves breaks as needed and then to go back into the image (for example, if someone is having to stand with stretched-out arms for a while).

- You may need to pay attention to the de-roling of participants, as you would with role-play exercises, if they have been holding frozen images for a particularly long time and/or you have been working on particularly difficult or painful experiences.

Working with conflict and challenge in the training room

As a facilitator and a trainer, there may be times when the behaviour of a participant challenges you. How you respond to these challenges will affect the outcomes of the training and participants' continuing engagement. When challenges are worked with creatively and constructively it can be an opportunity for everyone to learn (including facilitators), and for participants to deepen their understanding of youth and conflict issues. One of the advantages of having two facilitators is that when conflict or a challenge does occur, especially if it is directed at one of you, the other can step in and facilitate communication and group learning.

The most common types of challenge are:

INDIRECT CHALLENGES

These may not be voiced directly to you; however, you will be aware of them because of how someone is behaving. This behaviour may involve body language that indicates non-participation and engagement, for example looking repeatedly at their watch or the clock, yawning, whispering to others, arriving late, leaving early, complaining to other participants in breaks, and so on.

DIRECT CHALLENGES

These may be voiced out loud, either in front of the whole group or to you privately outside the session. They may involve a criticism of you in relation to your skills or knowledge as a facilitator or to the content of the training, or they may be a criticism of another participant, etc.

BEHAVIOUR THAT THREATENS THE SAFETY OF THE LEARNING ENVIRONMENT

Examples of this are if a participant behaves in an aggressive, rude or threatening manner to you or to participants, or if a participant is consistently late, or misses days or sections of days without explanation.

Strategies for working with conflict and challenge

PREPARATION

This will be your most effective strategy. By being thoroughly prepared, having clear intentions, instructions, timing and learning outcomes planned for all activities as well as having thought through the issues participants may bring to the training and being ready for these you will be composed and confident to apply consistently the frameworks and techniques of the training programme to situations arising in the room. This will allow you to work openly, creatively and constructively with any behaviour or comments that challenge you as a team or individually.

GROUP CONTRACT AND ENCOURAGING DIALOGUE

When making the group contract you can also invite participants to engage in dialogue with the facilitators whenever they find themselves struggling with an aspect of the course. By stating your commitment to participants' learning and to the maintenance of a supportive learning environment, and inviting them to enter into dialogue with you about the learning process, you will encourage them to take responsibility for their own learning.

WORKING WITHIN A FRAMEWORK OF AFFIRMATION AND VALUING EACH OTHER

It is important to work within a framework of affirmation, respect and value for each other. If you are consistently coming from this perspective in your interactions and engagement with participants then it will be easier to deal with any challenges that arise. It is especially important to remind yourself of this if one of you is being challenged very directly. By affirming the speaker for their honesty and directness and then asking questions to help you understand what it is exactly that they are saying it will be possible to assess the issues and respond appropriately.

NOT TAKING IT PERSONALLY

How you work with challenge as a facilitator will depend on the level of your facilitation experience and skills. The more opportunities you have to deal with challenge in the training room the more effective and comfortable you will become at working with it constructively and creatively. So, whilst it may feel uncomfortable in the moment it can be a real opportunity to develop your own skills further, and for the group to develop their understanding of working with challenge and conflict. If you take challenges personally it will make you less effective, and you will be more likely to close down the opportunities for learning, both for yourself and for participants.

WORKING FROM THE STANDPOINT THAT 'EVERYTHING IS USEFUL'

Working from the standpoint that everything that gets said in the training room is useful and an opportunity for everyone to learn can really support facilitators in working creatively with conflict and challenge. You can make it useful by helping participants to find the links with:

- the intention of the session
- the intention of previous sessions
- the participant's personal challenge or goal
- a particular framework or understanding around conflict, for example if someone in the group is reacting rather than responding (see Exercise 2.5, Reaction versus Response).

It may require you as a team to:

- notice your own expectations and hopes for how the session would go and be willing to let them go
- accept that the session will be different from how you pictured it
- work with what is happening in the room as opposed to trying to stick to the exact session plan.

WORKING WITH RESISTANCE OR INDIRECT CHALLENGE

If the behaviour is being carried out by one member of the group, one member of the facilitator team may speak to them privately in a break. The conversation might start with a question such as 'How are you finding the course?', followed with some observations on what you have noticed about how they are behaving in the training room. You may then ask them if there is anything you can do to support further their engagement in the training. Given the opportunity to have this conversation in an affirming and matter-of-fact way, participants are usually able to articulate the difficulties they are experiencing. It may also be that a participant is not able to engage with the training because of issues that they are dealing with outside the training room, for example, at home.

If there are a significant number of participants demonstrating indirect or resistant behaviour you may do the following:

- Do a whip-round or go-round asking participants how they are doing with the course. This is less direct but can be a good quick way of gauging where participants are at. Sometimes what you are picking up and interpreting as resistance can be participants needing a break or being too hot/cold/hungry/sleepy, etc.
- Address the behaviour directly by saying what you think you are noticing and following it up with questions that invite an open response. If you do this then you will need to feel confident as a team in dealing with whatever may come up.

RESPONDING TO A DIRECT CHALLENGE

Depending on the nature of the challenge you may respond in any or all of the following ways:

- You may be able to use the challenge as a way of supporting the participant around their personal challenge or goal. In this case you might use questions in order to encourage the participant to reflect on their behaviour and deepen their learning. We find it useful to initially summarise and reflect back to the challenger their first statements so that they are more likely to feel they have been heard, before bringing in questions of your own.

- Similarly, if the participant's challenge relates to the intentions and learning outcome of the workshop you might use the same techniques to encourage the participant to deepen their learning around the content of the workshop.

If neither of these feels appropriate to the challenge you could try one of the following:

- Ask the group 'Is that something others of you are experiencing?' In this way you can work out if the criticism is shared by others or particular to this one individual.

- Thank the participant for their feedback and say that you will return to them at a later point. This gives you some time to reflect on a response.

CONFLICT BETWEEN PARTICIPANTS

If there is conflict or disagreement between participants that is being inappropriately expressed there are a number of ways you can deal with it:

- If the conflict is not too hot you can use the tools and frameworks already shared on the programme to facilitate a greater understanding of the roots of the conflict and thereby support participants in finding some shared route forward.

- You may wish to remind participants of the group contract. You can also ask if anyone would like to comment on or add anything to the contract.

- You can ask the rest of the group to reflect on the behaviour and how it is affecting their ability to learn.

BEHAVIOUR THAT THREATENS THE SAFETY OF THE LEARNING ENVIRONMENT

Many of the strategies described above can be used to great effect, and usually the group's trust and learning is enhanced by having dealt successfully with a difficult or challenging situation.

However, on very rare occasions, an individual participant's behaviour can be such that it negatively impacts on the maintenance of a supportive learning environment and the learning and participation of other group members. In such cases it is incumbent on the facilitation team to ask the participant to leave the course. This is always a particularly difficult decision to make for facilitators and needs a lot of thought and reflection. You should not take this step without having tried most of the other strategies outlined above and both being in agreement that this is the most appropriate step to take. The conversation with the participant should take place privately and in a way that is affirming of them and free from anger or blame.

Although these situations can be difficult for group members too, they can also provide rich learning for a group about boundaries and strategies for identifying and dealing with unacceptable behaviour that can be taken forward into their own work practice.

The section 'Games and Group Discussion Techniques' provides further ideas for how to develop and maintain a safe and supportive learning environment in groups.

Programme evaluation

Individual written feedback sheets that check the participants' learning and experience against the programme's intentions should be used at the end of the course, and ideally a follow-up should be issued three to six months afterwards to gauge how practice has changed since participating in the course.

Leap has developed a robust system of evaluation of its youth programmes; it is anticipated that most youth work practitioners will have an organisational framework for evaluation that they can access.

Games and Group Discussion Techniques

Games

Here is a selection of the games that are part of the Leap Confronting Conflict trainer's toolkit. They are sorted into categories according to their use. Some belong to more than one category, for example, some of the warm-ups could also be used to introduce specific exercises. Part of the pleasure of using games is discovering how you can make the link between the game itself and the themes being covered in the session.

Categories

- **Icebreakers:** Games that can be used when a group first meets, to introduce people to each other and to start to break down initial inhibitions.

- **Warm-ups:** Games that can be played to warm up or energise a group, for example, at the start of the day. They can be played just for fun or you could debrief the group at the end, focusing on what participants have learned about themselves and conflict or on the skills they used in the game.

- **Lead-ins:** Games that lead in to specific activities or exercises. They can also be played on their own.

- **Energy changers:** Games that can be used to quieten a boisterous group (1 to 20, Tropical Rainstorm) or enliven a more sedate group (Zip Zap Boing, Touch Three Things).

- **Trust builders:** Games for building up group trust, awareness, cooperation and confidence. They demand extreme concentration. They should be introduced and facilitated with care, so that participants are fully aware of what they are about.

With any game, the safety of participants is paramount; you may want to add some rules (regarding physical contact, running, etc.) to minimise any risks due to the ages and/or levels of ability and disability of the group members. Most games can be adapted or modified to suit the needs of a particular group.

Icebreakers

HANDSHAKE

Everyone in the group stands up and moves round the room, shaking everyone else's hand and introducing themselves within a strict time limit of one minute. This gets energy up and obliges each participant to acknowledge everyone else.

ADJECTIVE NAMES

Sitting in a circle everyone introduces themselves one after the other, prefixing their name with an adjective which says something good about them. It can be as outrageously positive as they like – for example, Superb Sabir, Fantastic Fred, Animated Annie. The second person repeats the first person's adjective name and adds their own. The third person repeats the previous two, adding their own. And so on. The person who is last has the hardest job!

PATTERN NAME GAME

You will need three or four small beanbags or soft balls. Everyone stands in a circle. Begin with one beanbag which is thrown round the circle randomly. Each time it is caught the catcher says their own name. Keep this going until everyone has had a go. Now ask participants to call the name of the person to whom they are throwing as well, and keep this going until everyone has had a go. In the next round, everyone is thrown the bag just once. Participants stop saying their own names as they catch but continue to say the name of the person to whom they are throwing. When the round is completed, repeat it in exactly the same sequence. Each person only needs to remember who they receive the beanbag from and who they threw to last time. Halfway through this round introduce another bag, to be thrown in exactly the same sequence. You can continue adding more bags and see if the group can keep the pattern going.

The game can be further extended by having everyone move out of the circle and walk round the room. Participants must now be even more aware of who they receive and from who they throw to, while continuing the same sequence. If you really want to test people when the pattern is established reverse the order.

THE SUN SHINES ON

The participants sit in a large circle and you stand in the centre. Explain that you are standing in the sunshine and that they are sitting in the shade. In order to get a seat in the shade you need to say something that is true about you that everyone can see, for example, 'The sun shines on anyone with brown eyes.' If it is true about anyone sitting down they need to get up and change places, giving you a chance to take a seat. The person left standing then says something that is true about them and if it is true for anyone else they get up and change seats. Participants are not allowed to move to the seat on either side of them and have to keep moving out of their seat once they have started.

After a few turns change to something that is true about you that can't be seen, for example, a hidden talent, family, hobby etc. After a few more turns change to something that is true about you and conflict or about you and this course. At the end acknowledge participants' sharing and participation.

HOW DO YOU LIKE YOUR NEIGHBOURS?

The group sits in a circle. One person stands in the centre and asks someone sitting in the circle, 'How do you like your neighbours?' That person has two choices. They can say 'I like my neighbours just fine', in which case the two people sitting on either side of them have to get up and swap places whilst the person who has been standing in the centre tries to get into one of their seats. Alternatively, when asked, 'How do you like your neighbours?' the person sitting could say, 'I like my neighbours just fine but I would like to change them for...' and then call out the names of two other people in the group. The two neighbours need to get up and change places with the two new named people, whilst the person in the centre again tries to get a seat. Whoever is left standing takes the place in the centre of the circle.

Warm-ups

KNOCKY KNEES

You will need the same number of chairs as there are players, and a piece of A4 (letter) paper. Ask the participants to arrange the chairs around the room in a haphazard fashion at roughly equal distances from each other. One person volunteers to be Knocky Knees; they leave their chair and go to the furthest point in the room from their chair. They are only allowed to move with the piece of paper held between their knees. Their aim is to get a seat. They can occupy any chair that is free. Everyone else has to prevent them from getting a chair by occupying any empty chair around them. When they get a chair the person who has just come from that chair becomes the new Knocky Knees.

CAPTAIN, BOSUN, MATE

Participants need to be sitting in a circle. Ask for a volunteer to be the Captain. Players number off around the circle starting with the Captain and following with Bosun, Mate, Number 1, Number 2, and so on until everyone has a number or a rank. The aim of the game is to become Captain by catching the Captain out, so that you can be the one to give the orders. The Captain begins by saying, 'Captain to Bosun', then the Bosun says, 'Bosun to Mate', and then the Mate says, 'Mate to a number'. That person has to call their own number and then a number or rank to go next. You are not allowed to call the number on either side of you or bounce it back to the person who sent the message to you. If anyone makes a mistake they move to take up the chair of the highest number and everyone from their number or rank down has to move one seat and renumber themselves (the ranks and numbers go with the chairs, not with the people). Each round starts with 'Captain to Bosun; Bosun to Mate; Mate to…'. After everyone has got the hang of the game, you can make those people who make a mistake walk the plank and be out of the game; the game can continue until there are only five people left on the boat.

HOWDY, HOWDY, HOWDY

Participants stand in a circle. One person volunteers to start and they stand outside the circle. They walk round the circle and tap one person in the circle on the back. That person comes out of position and walks around the circle in the opposite direction to the person who tapped them. When the two meet, they must shake hands and say, 'Howdy, howdy, howdy' to each other before trying to get back to the space left in the circle by the person who was tapped. The first person back will fill the position; the other person will then be the tapper.

GRANDMOTHER'S KEYS

This is an adaptation of an old children's game. One person volunteers to be the grandmother. The grandmother stands at the end of the room looking towards the wall with her back to the rest of the group. Behind her, at her feet, is a large, jangly set of keys. The rest of the group move towards her slowly. Every time she turns round they freeze. If she sees anyone move they have to go back to the beginning. She gives no warning as to when she will turn round. The aim of the group is to retrieve the keys and get them back to the start without the grandmother seeing them. Once the keys have been grabbed each person has to touch them on their journey back to the beginning. If anyone is caught with them, the keys are returned to grandmother and the participant goes back to the beginning. A group will soon realise that the only way to achieve their aim is to work together and make sure that every time the grandmother turns around she is not able to tell who has the keys.

HURRICANE

You need multiples of 3 people plus 1 to play this game. Ask for three volunteers to demonstrate how the game will run. Two of them should stand about two feet apart, facing each other, and to raise their arms and rest their palms against each other's so they form an arch. The third person steps into the arch and stands in between them. The person in the middle is a door and those on either side are either a north wall or a south wall. They need to decide who is which wall. Ask everyone else to make up their houses like the demonstration model. The one person who is not in a house is the caller. They can call out doors, north walls or south walls – or any combination of those three. If they call out doors, all the doors have to change places and the caller will try to get in and be part of a house. If someone else is left out, they become the caller. If the caller does not get into a house, they will call again. They can also call out hurricane, in which case all the houses are blown apart, and people need to create new houses with new people. They can be whichever part of the house they like. Run the game for a number of rounds.

Lead-ins

FAST-MOTION FILM

In groups of three decide on a film you all know. You have three minutes to condense the main themes of the film into a one-minute performance. When the three minutes are up, the performances are viewed one at a time and the audience tries to identify the film.

A variation on this game is called Movie Freeze Frame. It is similar to Fast-motion Film but this time you have three minutes to show three still images from the film. As before the audience tries to identify the film.

These two variations are great lead-ins to role-play and tableau work.

MIME THE LIE

The group stands in a circle. The first person goes into the middle of the circle and mimes an action, such as mowing the lawn. The next person asks them what they are doing. They lie and say, for example, 'I'm feeding the dog.' The person who asked now goes into the circle and mimes whatever the previous person said. When the person next to them asks them what they are doing, they lie, and so the game continues until everyone has had a go in the middle of the circle. You can then reverse the order round the circle. You can also play a round where the whole group adds sound effects for the person miming.

This game can also be used as an introduction to role-play and to the Survival Game.

ELEPHANT, PALM TREE, HELICOPTER, DONKEY

Ask everyone to stand in a circle. Explain that the object of the game is for the person in the middle to catch someone out by pointing at them and shouting either 'Elephant', 'Palm Tree', 'Helicopter' or 'Donkey'. The participant who is pointed to has to get quickly into a physical sculpt of the character, joined by the people on either side of them. For example, the person at the centre of the elephant sculpts its head and trunk and the people on either side become the elephant's flapping ears. The person at the centre of the palm tree becomes the trunk and the people on either side are the waving branches of the tree. The person at the centre of the helicopter spins round with their arms outstretched to become the whirling blades, which the people on either side must avoid by ducking. The donkey must remain absolutely still and the people on either side must not move either.

Run through the game a couple of times, giving everyone a chance to become familiar with the different sculpts, before you start playing for real.

To start the game one person stands in the centre of the circle, points to any participant and calls out one of the characters, for example 'elephant'. That person and the two people on either side must immediately get into position, as described above, and freeze. If any of them hesitate or make a mistake, they become the caller in the centre of the circle and the caller will join the circle. This exercise can be used as a lead-in to tableau work.

MINGLE AND GRAB

Everyone walks round the room. You can vary the speed by calling out faster or slower. Every few minutes call out a number. Participants get into groups of whatever that number is and hold on to each other. Ask each group to make a physical representation of a given topic: for example, for pairs it could be Tom and Jerry; for threes it could be knife, fork and spoon; for groups of four it could be the seasons, and so on. The topics can be as creative as possible. It is good to call the number of the whole group at the end, so that everyone huddles as one group and creates a group picture.

This exercise can be used as a lead-in to tableau work.

JAILBREAK

This game requires an odd number of participants. Create a circle of chairs with enough chairs for half of the group to sit on, plus one empty chair. Half the group sit on the chairs. The trainer stands behind the empty chair; the rest of the group stand behind the other chairs. They are the prison warders. Each one has a prisoner to guard. The object of the game for the trainer is to fill their chair with a prisoner. The object for all the other warders is to prevent their prisoners from escaping from their prisons. The object of the game for the prisoners is to escape from their chairs to the one available empty prison. The trainer winks at one of the prisoners, who then tries to spring from their chair and cross over to the empty chair without being touched by their own warder. The warders keep their prisoners by tapping them on the shoulder after they move. They are not allowed to move their feet from a set position which is an arm's length behind the chair and they have to stand with their arms hanging loosely by their sides. Prisoners must sit with their backs touching the back of the chair. If a prisoner escapes, then the new warder with the empty chair has to try to get a new prisoner to their chair. After a time, all the participants swap roles – the warders become prisoners and the prisoners get a chance to be warders; one person will play a warder twice.

Energy changers

I TO 20

Sit in a circle and close your eyes. The group aims to count to 20 without deciding who says which number. Every time two people say the number at the same time they go back to the beginning again. It is actually easier to do with closed eyes, but if the group wants to start with their eyes open they may find they can make it work that way. Having extra rules can make it easier to start with (for instance, that each person is allowed to say only one number). As the group gets better at it, take away these rules and the group can find great satisfaction in succeeding.

TROPICAL RAINSTORM

Everyone stands in a tight circle with their eyes closed. The facilitator begins the storm by rubbing their hands together. The person on their right also starts rubbing their hands together. One by one, everyone copies the person to their left. Each individual does only what the person on their left does, regardless of what the facilitator is doing. Once the person on the left of the facilitator is rubbing their hands, the facilitator changes to clicking their fingers and this message is passed around the group. Each time the person on the left of the facilitator starts the action, the facilitator changes their activity moving through clapping, slapping their thighs and then stamping their feet. The storm abates in the opposite way to which it began – that is, from stamping to slapping to clapping, clicking and rubbing. The round ends with silence.

ZIP, ZAP, BOING

Ask everyone to stand in a circle. Tell them that you are going to pass the message 'zip' around the circle. Start by turning your head to the person on your right and saying 'zip'. They should then pass the message on by turning their head to the person on their right and saying 'zip'. This continues round the circle until it gets back to you. Then introduce two more concepts: 'zap' and 'boing'. If someone says 'zap' it changes the direction in which the message 'zip' is sent around the circle; so a person who is 'zipped' can reverse the order by turning back to the person who 'zipped' them and saying 'zap'. That person then continues with the 'zip' message travelling in the opposite direction. If someone says 'boing' they are passing the message to someone who is not next to them in the circle; they do this by pointing at another person with both their hands. The receiver then chooses which way to send the 'zip' round the circle. Whilst it may take a couple of goes for everyone to get the game, it is good fun when it gets going. If someone makes a mistake, the person next to them starts off the next round.

TOUCH THREE THINGS

This is a race to see how quickly participants can touch three named objects in the room. One person is the caller and stands in the middle of the room. Everyone mills around them. The caller names three things in the room, such as the blue chair, the windowsill and the light switch. Participants must touch them as quickly as they can, although not necessarily in that order. The last person to finish can call out the next list.

SHARKS

Use large pieces of newspaper to create 'islands' on the floor. Ask participants to move round the room avoiding the islands. Ask them to imagine that they are swimming in a lovely warm sea; at the moment the water is safe, but in a moment you are going to shout 'shark!' and they will need to get onto one of the islands.

Call 'shark' and all the participants should be able to easily get onto an island. Play several rounds of the game and with each round remove one of the islands so participants have to huddle together to save themselves and each other from the sharks. At the end of the game there will only be one island left; encourage participants to come up with creative ways of saving each other!

Trust games
WHERE SHALL WE GO?

Participants divide into pairs. One person in each pair is blindfolded. The seeing person asks them where they would like to go. This can be anywhere from a beach to a fairground or a party. It is entirely up to the person who is blindfolded. The seeing person holds them by the hand or arm and takes them on a walk round the room, guiding them physically through the imaginary landscape. It is up to the seeing person to describe exactly where they are and what they are doing.

WIND IN THE WILLOWS

Gather round in a tight circle. One person volunteers to go in the middle. They close their eyes and allow themselves to fall, keeping their body straight, and the others catch and support them. (Supporters hold hands up in front and stand with one leg slightly in front of the other with knees bent. This is the strongest possible position.) Initially the group should stand fairly close in so that the person need not feel they are falling far. As confidence grows, the people in the group can move away a little. Take turns and give everyone the opportunity to have a go. Take care that there are plenty of people able to hold someone up, especially if there is a heavier person in the middle.

WALKING BLINDFOLD

Everyone stands in a large circle. One person volunteers to be blindfold and is taken to the middle of the circle. From there they can walk in any direction and when they get to the edge of the circle the nearest person gently takes hold of them and redirects them. Make sure there is time for everyone to have a turn at being blindfold.

THROUGH THE RUSHES

Participants stand in two lines facing each other, far enough apart for their outstretched arms to meet and slightly overlap. One by one each participant moves to one end, closes their eyes and walks between the two lines. The person walking through the two lines should have to push very slightly against the outstretched arms. It can be a very relaxing sensation.

RUNNING BLINDFOLD

Stand all the participants at one end of the room. One person volunteers to be blindfold and stands at the other end of the room. They run to the end where the group are standing. The group must be prepared to catch the running person gently. They should stand in a half-moon shape and shout stop before the runner reaches them. Initially people anticipate reaching the end of the room and begin to slow down. Encourage people to run as fast as they can until the group shouts stop, and to trust that the group really will make sure they don't hit the wall.

Group discussion techniques

In 'Guidance for Trainers', the section on working with conflict and challenge in the training room introduces strategies to consider when you are challenged by the behaviour of a particular participant. This section introduces a number of group discussion techniques that you can use to encourage dialogue, get problems out in the open and break an impasse when difficulties or conflicts have arisen in the group as well as some activities that will enable you to explore the impact of particular behaviours in the group more widely.

Some of the activities will challenge the listening skills of the participants; it is suggested that they will have already completed work on listening. You might also want to consider how the mediation skills developed in Chapter 7, Mediation and Action for Change, can be used in a group situation.

WORDSTORM

This is a quick technique for gathering a range of ideas from the group. Write a statement such as: 'Conflict is…' in the middle of a piece of flipchart paper. Ask participants to call out their immediate responses. These are all recorded on the flipchart. Single words or short phrases are best. All contributions are accepted – where a suggestion is not clear or appears not to be relevant, the facilitator can ask the speaker one or two questions to clarify their intention. Nobody offers criticism or judgement. Wordstorming is an inclusive way of getting an immediate impression of the range of responses in the group and can produce material to develop further.

WHIP-ROUND

Introduce the subject, for example, an observation or an issue from the previous session. Going clockwise round the circle, each participant responds to the subject. Everyone else listens without comment. The aim of the exercise is to get a quick gathering of points of view or observations rather than the participants making long statements. There is no discussion – whatever a person chooses to offer is valid. It is an affirmative and supportive practice, allowing people to express their feelings without question or judgement.

Variations on this exercise include asking people for their hopes and fears about an activity or event or their thoughts and feelings about a particular experience.

THE TALKING STICK

Place a fairly substantial object in the middle of the circle – this is the talking stick. Introduce the topic or problem to address. When anyone wants to talk, they have to go to the centre of the circle, pick up the object and return with it to their seat before they can start speaking. Once they have the object they can speak for as long as they like and say as much or as little as they like. The speaker returns the object to the middle when they have finished. Everyone should have a turn at holding the object. If they do not wish to speak while holding it they do not need to do so. The aim is to create a safe environment in which feelings and thoughts can be expressed without the need to justify their opinions. There should be no comeback from anyone once a point has been made. Individuals can respond to what someone else has said, but not by dismissing or rubbishing their contribution.

THE INNER CIRCLE

Place three chairs in the middle of the circle. Appoint a timekeeper and adjudicator for the exercise. Identify the topic for discussion and then invite up to three people to fill the chairs. Not all the chairs have to be filled to start the discussion. Only the participants in the three chairs in the middle may speak. Each may do so twice at most, for no longer than three minutes at a time. They may speak for the second time only when the other two participants have spoken at least once and, once they have spoken twice, they need to leave their chair and return to the outer circle. If someone from the outer circle wishes to speak, they should approach someone in the middle who has spoken at least once and tap them on the shoulder. Each speaker should address their contributions to the other seated participants. No comments should be personally directed. Decide when it is appropriate to end the discussion – it might be useful to ask the group if they think they have fully explored the topic.

CIRCLE PROBLEM SOLVE

This exercise can be used to cooperatively resolve a particular problem or issue within the group. Ask a member of the group to articulate their problem or concern. The person on the left of the speaker needs to clarify what they have said by reflecting back, 'Meena, you said…' The speaker confirms the problem has been accurately heard. The person on the left of the second speaker now opens the problem out to the rest of the group by saying, 'A member of the group feels that…' so that the problem becomes depersonalised and becomes a problem for the whole group to solve. The next person in the circle now defines the task, trying to suggest an approach that takes into account all sides of the problem. The next speaker makes a suggestion about how the problem could be resolved (it should be a suggestion, not a prescription). The discussion proceeds round the circle, with each person building on what has previously been said until a solution is reached. It is important to check that members of the group agree with the decision.

A variation on this exercise is to allow speakers to change the direction the discussion is travelling in; they must first summarise what has been said to date, then give their reasons for disagreeing and suggest a new direction. The following speaker can choose whether to follow this direction or return to the original proposal.

IN SOMEONE ELSE'S SHOES

Ask participants to write down two statements, one on each side of a small index card, in response to two related questions, for example, 'In what way do you feel appreciated and valued by the group?' and 'In what way do you feel unappreciated and undervalued by the group?' The statements could also be in response to a specific theme or problem. If participants know each other well, or if the subject is very sensitive, you could take the statements away and type them up during a break. Redistribute the cards amongst the group, ensuring each member has a card written by someone else. In pairs, the partners read their cards to one another, interpreting them as if they were their own, so as to gain an understanding of the points of view they themselves might not share. Then bring the participants back into the circle and ask each one to read out what was on their card as if it were their own and give a short explanation about it.

The exercise can be developed further by exploring the information that has been shared, both the original statements and the explanations given as to why someone wrote it. It has been used successfully to create group trust and understanding; to help resolve group disputes; to assist in the gathering of sensitive information in an unthreatening way; and to help in the resolution of a conflict between two groups, such as management and staff.

ME IN ACTION

This exercise can be used when some of the participants' behaviours in the group are causing difficulties or tensions. Ask participants to note down their most common ways of operating within a group situation. You can write up a list of questions for them to consider: Why do you think you behave in this way? Is there pressure on you to behave like this? What are the pay-offs for you – what do you gain from that behaviour? What might be the impact of these behaviours on the group – what might be the costs of the behaviour? In pairs, ask people to share what they have written down and then to pick one behaviour they would like to change. In pairs, participants help each other formulate a clear statement about what it is they would like to change. The participants share their statements with the whole group. The facilitator can work with participants to ensure the statements are clear and identify ways they can support them in meeting their challenge.

STICKING TO THE POINT

Divide participants into groups of four. The group selects someone to speak and someone to act as timekeeper and adjudicator. The speaker picks a subject to speak about, for example, 'My family'. They will talk for one minute on their chosen topic. The other two members will listen closely and call out any of the following 'offences' if they feel the speaker has been 'guilty' of them: repetition (unnecessary reiteration of facts or details); digression (anything off the point or irrelevant to the subject matter); or hesitation (any lengthy pause in the delivery). If the listeners call out any of these offences, the speaker stops and the timekeeper adjudicates as to whether an offence has indeed been committed. Then the clock is restarted (the timekeeper should ideally have a stopwatch) and the speaker continues until they are stopped again or the minute is up. The timekeeper keeps a record of how many legitimate calls were made during the minute and what the offences were. Everyone in the group should speak on their own topic, and the role of timekeeper/adjudicator should also rotate. Explore with participants their experience of taking part in the activity and what they have learned about the way they express themselves. How might this impact on the group dynamics?

PRAISE, CRITICISM OR FEEDBACK?

Distribute a selection of index cards face down to the group. On each card you will have written a short phrase offering praise, criticism or feedback. Examples might include 'You're great', 'You're stupid', 'You spoke very clearly', etc. Go round and ask each person to look at their card and in turn say the statement on their card to the group with the tone, volume and expression with which they associate it. The group will then decide if what they have heard is praise, criticism or feedback. Ask them to think about the feelings and thoughts that come up in relation to each phrase, and how someone might act if they experience that. You can record their answers. It is likely that their focus will be on receiving praise, criticism or feedback rather than on giving them to others. In pairs ask the participants to identify their own habits around giving praise, criticism or feedback to others. Ask them to consider if they have been operating in that way within this group. Invite the group to share back from their pairs. It may be that this creates an opportunity to clear up any mistakes or make requests or suggestions in the group. If so, encourage the group to use 'I' statements to practise a clean, clear way of communicating.

Note: Feedback is information – we have a choice about whether we receive it as a gift or a put-down. Effective feedback focuses on the deed, not the doer. When we are giving feedback it is important to acknowledge that our words have an impact and the way we frame and deliver it makes a difference to how it is heard.

Appendix A

Example Programmes and Session Plans

A ten-day intensive course

Each training day on the course runs from 10am until 5pm with two 20-minute breaks morning and afternoon and a one-hour lunch break. Exercises from the chapters are in bold; all the other activities are explained in 'Guidance for Trainers'. The timings of exercises may need to be modified to fit the training day.

Weekend One: Me in Conflict	
DAY 1	
Activity	*Duration*
Course Set-up	60 min.
Game	15 min.
Group contract	25 min.
Focus of the day	10 min.
1.1 Personal Road Maps	45 min.
Gathering	10 min.
Game	15 min.
1.4 Conflict Line-up	60 min.
2.3 Bombs and Shields	10 min.
2.4 Red Flags	35 min.
Introduction to buddies and buddy time	15 min.
Journal time	10 min.
Evaluation and closing	10 min.

DAY 2	
Activity	*Duration*
Welcome back	10 min.
Recap yesterday	10 min.
Clearing	30 min.
Focus of the day	5 min.
Game	15 min.
2.5 Reaction versus Response	20 min.
Fire and Conflict Model	15 min.
1.5 Testing the Water	10 min.
Personal challenges	50 min.
Gathering	5 min.
Game	10 min.
3.5 Thought Patterns	45 min.
4.12 The Survival Game	65 min.
Buddy time	10 min.
Journal time	10 min.
Evaluation and closing	10 min.

DAY 3	
Activity	*Duration*
Welcome back	10 min.
Recap yesterday	5 min.
Clearing	30 min.
Focus of the day	5 min.
Game	15 min.
4.1 Statements of Anger	25 min.
4.2 Emotion Pictures	15 min.
4.3 Statues of Anger	20 min.
4.4 Underlying Anger	35 min.
Gathering	10 min.
Game	20 min.
2.11 Find Your Voice	25 min.
4.5 Yes/No	10 min.
4.6 Facing Anger	65 min.
Buddy time	10 min.
Journal time	10 min.
Evaluation and closing	10 min.

DAY 4	
Activity	*Duration*
Welcome back	10 min.
Recap yesterday	5 min.
Clearing	30 min.
Focus of the day	5 min.
Game	10 min.
3.10 Greet, Argue, Make Up	15 min.
3.11 Attack and Avoid	40 min.
3.8 You or I?	20 min.
3.9 'I' Statements (introduction)	15 min.
Gathering	10 min.
Game	10 min.
3.9 'I' Statements (continued)	30 min.
7.8 The Boxing Ring	70 min.
Reflection time	20 min.
Buddy time	10 min.
Journal time	10 min.
Evaluation and closing	10 min.

Weekend Two: You and Me in Conflict	
DAY 5	
Activity	*Duration*
Welcome back	10 min.
Game	10 min.
Recap	45 min.
Focus of the day	5 min.
Stages of conflict (fire and conflict analogy)	20 min.
3.12 Situations 1–5	50 min.
1.8 Countdown	20 min.
Gathering	10 min.
Game	20 min.
1.9 Attention Zones	35 min.
7.3 Facts and Feelings	30 min.
1.10 What Language Do You Speak?	25 min.
Reflection time	10 min.
Buddy time	10 min.
Journal time	10 min.
Evaluation and closing	10 min.

DAY 6	
Activity	*Duration*
Welcome back	10 min.
Recap yesterday	5 min.
Clearing	30 min.
Focus of the day	5 min.
Game	10 min.
5.1 Pam, Reggie and Vernon	30 min.
5.2 The Power Game	45 min.
4.7 Enemy Thinking	10 min.
4.8 My Enemy	30 min.
Gathering	10 min.
Game	20 min.
4.9 Personal Projection	20 min.
4.10 Facing Projection from Others	60 min.
Wind-down game	15 min.
Buddy time	10 min.
Journal time	10 min.
Evaluation and closing	10 min.

DAY 7	
Activity	*Duration*
Welcome back	10 min.
Recap yesterday	5 min.
Clearing	30 min.
Focus of the day	5 min.
Game	10 min.
3.1 Sharing Power	30 min.
3.2 Statues of Power or **3.3 Positional versus Personal Power**	30 min.
5.6 Breaking the Code	25 min.
5.5 Dominant and Subordinate Groups (introduction)	25 min.
Gathering	5 min.
Game	15 min.
5.5 Dominant and Subordinate Groups (continued)	20 min.
5.7 Privilege	40 min.
Using materials with young people	50 min.
Buddy time	10 min.
Journal time	10 min.
Evaluation and closing	10 min.

Weekend Three: You, Me and Others in Conflict	
DAY 8	
Activity	*Duration*
Welcome back	10 min.
Recap last weekend	75 min.
Focus of the day	5 min.
Game	10 min.
6.1 Throwing the Stone	65 min.
Gathering	10 min.
Game	15 min.
6.6 What's My Role?	30 min.
7.1 Introduction to Mediation	30 min.
6.3 Mapping a Conflict	40 min.
Buddy time	10 min.
Journal time	10 min.
Evaluation and closing	10 min.

DAY 9	
Activity	*Duration*
Welcome back	10 min.
Recap yesterday	5 min.
Clearing	20 min.
Focus of the day	5 min.
Game	10 min.
6.5 Positions, Interests, Needs	20 min.
7.2 Questioning	30 min.
7.4 Behind the Scenes	35 min.
7.5 Words Unheard	35 min.
Gathering	10 min.
Game	15 min.
7.6 Acting Impartially	45 min.
7.7 Mediation in the Moment	50 min.
Reflection time	10 min.
Buddy time	10 min.
Journal time	10 min.
Evaluation and closing	10 min.

DAY 10	
Activity	*Duration*
Welcome back	10 min.
Recap yesterday	5 min.
Clearing	25 min.
Focus of the day	5 min.
Game	10 min.
6.8 My Vision	60 min.
6.9 From Present to Future	55 min.
Gathering	10 min.
Game	10 min.
7.9 Conflict in Action or **7.12 Action for Change**	40 min.
6.11 Support Yourself	40 min.
Buddy time	10 min.
Journal time	10 min.
Evaluation	10 min.
Closing	20 min.

Suggestions for themed sessions or short courses

Internal and personal intervention

Exploring anger	Exploring thoughts
2.3 Bombs and Shields	3.7 Positive and Negative Thoughts
2.4 Red Flags	3.5 Thought Patterns
4.1 Statements of Anger	3.4 Hidden Thoughts
4.3 Statues of Anger	3.6 Describing a Habit
4.4 Underlying Anger	
4.6 Facing Anger	

Exploring patterns of behaviour	Exploring power
1.1 Personal Road Maps	3.1 Sharing Power
4.1 Statements of Anger	3.2 Statues of Power
4.8 My Enemy	3.3 Positional versus Personal Power
4.9 Personal Projection	5.1 Pam, Reggie and Vernon
	5.2 The Power Game

Developing personal intervention strategies	Developing personal resources
2.7 Immediate Responses	1.10 What Language Do You Speak?
2.8 Three to One	2.10 States of Tension
3.12 Situations 1–5	2.11 Find Your Voice
3.9 'I' Statements	2.12 Voice and Energy for Change
	2.9 Slow Motion
	3.11 Attack and Avoid

Second-party intervention

Exploring identity and prejudice	Developing communication
5.3 Assumptions Quiz	1.12 Reading the Face
5.4 Identity Shields	1.10 What Language Do You Speak?
5.5 Dominant and Subordinate Groups	1.11 Open and Closed
5.6 Breaking the Code	1.9 Attention Zones
5.7 Privilege	1.7 Back-to-back Listening
5.8 Culture Pyramid	1.8 Countdown
2.6 Red Labels	
5.9 History of the Word	

5.10 Reclaiming or Sustaining	
5.11 Defining Inappropriate Language	
5.12 Challenge Carousel	

Third-party intervention

Developing mediation skills	Exploring actual or potential group conflict
7.1 Introduction to Mediation	6.1 Throwing the Stone
7.2 Questioning	6.2 Conflict Timeline
7.3 Facts and Feelings	6.3 Mapping a Conflict
7.4 Behind the Scenes	6.4 The ABC Triangle
7.5 Words Unheard	6.5 Positions, Interests, Needs
7.6 Acting Impartially	7.9 Conflict in Action
7.7 Mediation in the Moment	

Appendix B
References

Acland, A. (1990) *A Sudden Outbreak of Common Sense*. London: Hutchinson Business Books.

Allport, G. (1954) *The Nature of Prejudice*. Boston, MA: Beacon Press.

Burnard, P. (1994) *Counselling Skills for Health Professionals* (2nd edition). London: Chapman & Hall.

Fisher, S., Abdi, D.I., Ludin, J., Smith, R., Williams, S. and Williams, S. (1998) *Working with Conflict: Skills and Strategies for Action*. London: Zed Books in association with Responding to Conflict.

Karpman, S. (1968) 'Fairy tales and script drama analysis.' *Transactional Analysis Bulletin 7*, 26, 39–43.

Kolb, D. (1984) *Experiential Learning: Experience as the Source of Learning and Development*. Upper Saddle River, NJ: Prentice Hall.

Lifelong Learning UK (2007) *National Occupational Standards for Youth Work*. Available at www.lluk.org/wp-content/uploads/2010/11/National-Occupational-Standards-for-Youth-Work.pdf, accessed on 17 March 2011.

Loden, M. (1996) *Implementing Diversity*. New York: McGraw-Hill.

Sharp, G. (1973) *The Politics of Nonviolent Action, Part 2: The Methods of Nonviolent Action*. Westford, MA: Porter Sargent.

Appendix C
Useful Websites and Further Reading

Websites and organisations

Leap Confronting Conflict

www.leapconfrontingconflict.org.uk

Leap Confronting Conflict is a UK specialist in youth and conflict work.

Theatre of the Oppressed

www.theatreoftheoppressed.org

This site covers the range of theatrical forms that were elaborated and developed by the Brazilian theatre practitioner Augusto Boal in the 1950s and 1960s.

Geese Theatre

www.geesetheatre.com

Geese Theatre is a drama theatre company developing experiential theatre and therapy in 42 USA states and 9 countries. Their site provides a valuable resource for training in drama therapy within the prison context: for offices, for adult and young offenders and for those running theatre in prisons.

Responding to Conflict

www.respond.org

Responding to Conflict is a non-governmental organisation that works to transform conflict and build peace. This site provides advice, cross-cultural training and longer-term support to people working for peace in societies affected or threatened by violent conflict.

School Mediation Associates

www.schoolmediation.com

School Mediation Associates helped create the peer mediation concept 25 years ago. As part of their mission they are committed to transforming schools into safer, more caring and more effective institutions.

Conflict Resolution Network

www.crnhq.org

Conflict Resolution Network offers conflict resolution skills to build stronger organisations and more rewarding relationships. The site provides books, trainers' manuals, audio and video tapes, DVDs and posters in conflict resolution and related communication skills.

Commission on Integration and Cohesion

www.integrationandcohesion.org.uk

This site provides the final report of the Commission on Integration and Cohesion established in 2007. *Our Shared Future* considers how local areas can make the most of diversity whilst being able to respond to the underlying tension this may cause. It is accompanied by a compendium of good practice, case studies and research reflecting on the commission's focus.

The Freire Institute

www.freire.org

The Freire Institute is a community-based learning organisation. This site provides a platform for practitioners to attend, practise and understand Paulo Freire's concepts on global education. Freire uses a 'social knowledge' approach.

Further reading

Working with conflict

Cornelius, H. and Faire, S. (2006) *Everyone Can Win: Responding to Conflict Constructively* (2nd edition). Pymble, NSW, Australia: Simon & Schuster.

Deutsch, M., Coleman, P. and Marcus, E.C. (2006) *The Handbook of Conflict Resolution: Theory and Practice.* San Francisco, CA: Jossey-Bass.

Lederach, J.P. (2003) *The Little Book of Conflict Transformation.* Intercourse, PA: Good Books.

Rosenberg, M. (2003) *Nonviolent Communication: A Language of Life* (2nd edition). Encinitas, CA: PuddleDancer Press.

Working with young people

Bannister, A. and Huntington, A. (2002) *Communicating with Children and Adolescents: Action for Change.* London: Jessica Kingsley Publishers.

Broadwood, J. and Carmichael, H. (1996, 1999) *Tackling Bullying: Conflict Resolution with Young People.* London: LBTH Learning Design.

Feinstein, J. and Imani Kuumba, N. (2006) *Working with Gangs and Young People.* London: Jessica Kingsley Publishers.

Harrison, R. and Wise, C. (2005) *Working with Young People.* London: Sage Publications Ltd.

Working with diversity

Clements, P. and Jones, J. (2006) *The Diversity Training Handbook* (2nd edition). London: Kogan Page.

Dalrymple, J. and Burke, B. (2003) *Anti-oppressive Practice, Social Care and the Law.* Maidenhead: Open University Press.

Lewis, M. and Newman, N. (2007) *Challenging Attitudes, Perceptions and Myths*. London: IPPR Publications.

Parekh, B. (2000) *Rethinking Multiculturalism: Cultural Diversity and Political Theory*. Cambridge, MA: Harvard University Press.

Vertovec, S. (2007) *New Complexities of Cohesion in Britain*. Oxford: ESRC Centre on Migration, Policy and Society (COMPAS), University of Oxford.

Working with groups

Cottrell, S. (2005) *Critical Thinking Skills*. Basingstoke: Palgrave Macmillan.

Freire, P. (1972) *Pedagogy of the Oppressed*. Harmondsworth: Penguin.

Goleman, D. (2005) *Emotional Intelligence*. New York, NY: Bantam Books

Hogan, C. (2002) *Understanding Facilitation: Theory and Principle*. London: Kogan Page.

Johnson, D.W. and Johnson, F.P. (2005) *Joining Together: Group Theory and Group Skills*. London: Pearson/Allyn & Bacon.

Using arts in conflict

Baime, C., Brookes, S. and Mountford, A. (2002) *The Geese Theatre Handbook*. Winchester: Waterside Press.

Boal, A. (1985) *Theatre of the Oppressed*. New York, NY: Theatre Communications Group.

Boal, A. (1992) *Games for Actors and Non Actors*. London: Routledge.

Herrmann, A. and Clifford, S. (1999) *Making A Leap: Theatre of Empowerment*. London: Jessica Kingsley Publishers.

Liebmann, M. (1996) *Arts Approaches to Conflict*. London: Jessica Kingsley Publishers.

Negotiation

Fisher, R., Ury, W. and Patten, B. (2003) *Getting to Yes: Negotiating Agreement without Giving In* (revised 2nd edition). London: Penguin Putnam.

Ury, W. (1992) *Getting Past No: Negotiating with Difficult People*. New York: Bantam Books.

Mediation

Beer, J. with Stief, E. (1997) *The Mediator's Handbook*. Gabriola Island, BC: New Society Publishers.

Baruch Bush, R. and Folger, J. (2005) *The Promise of Mediation* (revised edition). San Francisco, CA: Jossey-Bass.

Mennonite Conciliation Service (2000) *Mediation and Facilitation Training Manual*. Akron, PA: Mennonite Conciliation Service.

Working in the wider community

Hopkins, B. (2004) *Just Schools: A Whole School Approach to Restorative Justice*. London: Jessica Kingsley Publishers.

Ury, W. (2000) *The Third Side* (revised edition). New York, NY: Penguin Putnam.